How Elaine's books have helped others since 2003...

"An amazing book brimming with ideas for military families. Fuel for the fire of passion we call our military lives. We believe in Elaine's work so much we've made it a part of our Spouse Field Exercise Conferences!"

– Tara Crooks and Star Henderson
www.FieldProblems.com and co-hosts
www.ArmyWifeTalkRadio.com

"Thank you so much for all the ideas, hints and helps in your book. I'm getting excited for my husband to return from this deployment. I have so many things that I plan to use from your book to show him how I have thought of him while he has been away. I have a lot to do now!! As a Command Ombudsman for over 2½ years, I referred to your book many times to help me with situations with the spouses and family members. It's been a GREAT resource."

– Julie Doyle

"I wish I had this book at the beginning of my marriage to a soldier. It would have made the many deployments a much different experience. I think as military wives, we need to use all the tools available to help us cope with our special circumstances."

– M. Fichtner, the forever loyal wife of a
Special Forces soldier

"You're doing a great thing with this book. I, along with hundreds of thousands thank you for bringing light to this lifestyle. It is nothing glamorous but it is most rewarding in the end. I appreciate your work and devotion!"

– OS1 Timothy Mollock, USN

"In skimming through part of the book, some of the things in it brought me to tears; and there were some of your wonderful ideas that I'd like to employ with my own children with their dad having recently been gone a lot more on business trips. Thank you for taking the time to do this ministry!"

– Charlene Johnson (via email)

"Today the reality of how much your book has helped hit when a lady emailed me (I am coordinator of our family support group) asking for help with her children whose daddy is deployed in Iraq now. All the ideas that I gave her came from your book! What joy it was to pass along quality information that worked wonders in our home."

– Jeannette (via email)

"My sister discovered your book and ordered a copy for me. My husband has now deployed for the second time in less than two years. He is now in Iraq. My sincerest thanks to you for putting together such a wonderful and inspirational resource. Your ideas help ease some of the loneliness for me."

– Kelly Ayala (via email)

"What a heart-touching book. I am amazed at the creativity and compassion exhibited in these examples! Makes me want to do something special for my kids tonight."

— Laura Benjamin – seven year Veteran of the US Air Force (enlisted)

"I love this book! I have wanted something like this for years. My mother bought it for me as a wonderful token for the upcoming deployment we have later this month. I can't praise it enough. I love the diverse backgrounds that all the ideas are from and their different points of view. It makes the book even that much more interesting. Thank you for putting this book together."

— Ashley Klein, "1st cav" fan

"After reading your book it became obvious to me that several of my men's wives must have used your tips while we were deployed in Afghanistan. These guys always had a smile on their faces and were the envy of the base. Thanks for making our stay overseas that much more bearable!"

— CPT Diggs Brown, USSF, author of
Your Neighbor Went to War

"As a military spouse one is never alone. There are countless sources of aid and guidance available. *I'm Already Home* is one of the most creative and comprehensive."

— Captain Gerald Coffee, US Navy (Ret.)...
P.O.W. North Vietnam, seven years

"I cannot say enough about wonderful people like you who have insight to the military life and know how much it means to us that the American people care. You hear so much about the negative side and it's nice to know, hear and see someone non-military who is involved to support the troops and their families."

– Jo Ann Cherry, Alabama FRG and
military wife

"Your book is absolutely wonderful! As you can see, I am all over it. This is indeed one for Oprah!"

– V. Palmer, New Jersey (via email)

"I wholeheartedly endorse the book and the many ways, so simple, that anyone can use those great ideas to just put that smile on the face of their loved one, at perhaps just the right moment. It gives them hope, happiness, and knowledge that their relationship is so vital."

– Janet Weber, MSG MIARNG

"Thank you for your 'ministry.' It is a great support to military families. When our son went to Iraq a couple of years ago, we got your book with ideas of things to do to help the children (and parents) cope and still feel close."

– Colene Read, Kansas

The Road Home –

Smoothing the transition back from deployment

Elaine Gray Dumler

Published by Frankly Speaking, Inc.
Westminster, Colorado

೧

Care has been taken to ensure that the information in this book
was accurate at the time of publication.
Be advised that addresses, phone numbers, email addresses, etc.,
may change, and that companies may go out of business
or change their products and services.
We are happy to receive corrections, comments and suggestions
for future editions.
This book is intended for use with adult supervision.
The reader assumes all responsibility for any actions taken
as a result of anything contained in this book.
The author and publisher shall have neither liability nor responsibility
to any person or entity with respect to any mishaps or damage caused,
or alleged to be caused, directly or indirectly by the
information contained in this book.

೧

Published by Frankly Speaking, Inc.
6460 W. 98th Court, Westminster, CO 80021 • 303-430-0592

Elaine@ElaineDumler.com

www.ImAlreadyHome.com

೧

The Road Home –
Smoothing the transition back from deployment
Elaine Gray Dumler
ISBN: 978-0-9740359-2-5

Printed in the United States of America
Library of Congress Control Number: 2009900617

About the Cover

The quilt on the cover is special because it's designed by national quilt designer Pepper Cory and lovingly pieced by the women in her guild, Mary Frankle, Mary Henris, and Jan Spickett. I knew the quilt was a perfect match because the design name is The Road Home! The beautiful custom quilting was done by Marine wife and mother, and longarm quilter Lori Housel of Colorado. You can read more about the story behind the quilt, see full photographs and get information on the pattern at www.ImAlreadyHome.com.

The photograph on the quilt is by U.S. Air Force SSgt. Thomas J. Sobczyk, Jr. and is used with permission of both the photographer and the wonderful family portrayed in the picture. Meet the Hoffmanns: Lt Col Pete Hoffmann is from the Wisconsin Air National Guard's 128th Air Refueling Wing, and is embracing his family upon his return from Operation Enduring Freedom.

Cover design and layout by:
Kerri Lian with MacGraphics
Aurora, Colorado
www.macgraphics.net

Quilt Design by:
Pepper Cory
www.peppercory.com
General quilting blog:
http://peppercory.blogspot.com
Quilt Flap blog:
http://quiltflapper.blogspot.com

Quilt custom quilted by:
Lori Housel
The Quilting Heart
11704 Memphis Street
Commerce City, Colorado 80022
303-989-0025
lorihousel@msn.com

Cover photo and inside author photo taken by:
Joyce Jay
303-420-8533

Back cover family photo taken by freelance photographer:
Dan Greenberg
Dan@photoart101.com
www.photoart101.com
www.pbase.com/dlgphoto

Edited by:
Denise Hmieleski
Denisehmi@me.com
P.O. Box 709
Lafayette, Colorado 80026-0709

Page layout by:
Laura Vincent, BOSS Printing
Broomfield, Colorado

Acknowledgements

I am grateful to many people who helped with this book. Thanks to Suzanne Buemi, Charlene Shields and the entire Colorado National Guard Family Readiness office who provided information, articles, resources, and a great deal of friendship!

I've enjoyed working with designer Pepper Cory on the quilt for the cover of the book. Most of you know I'm a quilter, so it seemed natural that a special quilt would represent the Welcome Home we extend to all our deployed service members. I'm so grateful to Lori Housel for generously providing the quilting on this beautiful piece. She does wonderful work and would love to longarm quilt your projects for you.

I can never repay Denise Hmieleski for the amazing editing job. You made my words actually sound like I wanted them to!

Thank you to the members of my Mastermind group: Fred Berns, Sarah Michel, Jay Arthur, Brad Montgomery, and LeAnn Thieman. You all remained faithful cheerleaders and are more important to me than you know.

Thanks to my wonderful office assistant Jenn Shumate who put together the resources and support section for you but also kept me on track to get this finished!

Special thanks goes out to Matt Eversmann, Erin Richardson, Rick, Debbie, and Kyle Anderson, Linda

Engleman, Jenn Shumate, Crystal Strain and Lawrence Luck for your care and special understanding of the needs of the families, and for sharing your words and your hearts with us. Thanks to the hundreds of other amazing military family members for sharing your ideas with me and making me feel like I was invited into your living rooms. I thank all the wonderful volunteers at Family Readiness and Support Centers for all the work you do and for being the vehicles for getting this book into the hands of the families it can help.

Finally, I thank God for planting the vision of all three books in my heart and selecting me to be the messenger for helping military families stay strong.

Dedication

This book is dedicated to my husband (Larry) and
my son (Bryan) who showed me
how rewarding it is to raise kids.
And to my parents (Ralph and Josie),
sisters (Rondi and Nancy), and brother (Brad)
where I learned about love and laughter
from the beginning—even in the tough times.

Beyond the dedication, this book
wouldn't have been written without the
emotional inspiration that came from
my sister Nancy (Early) and her
wonderful family (Jim, Stacy and Kenny).
When Nancy lost her battle with cancer,
her family showed more love and support
than I thought was possible.
They were also an inspiration to many
who were around them during that time.
I love you.

Table of Contents

Foreword

I enlisted into the Army in 1987. Ronald Reagan had just put the finishing touches on the Russians and ended the Cold War. It was hard for me to imagine serving my enlistment with no prevalent enemy to fight and no battlefields to conquer.

In 1989, while I was in the U.S. Army Ranger School at Ft. Benning, U.S. forces invaded Panama to rid the country of its brutal dictator, Manuel Noriega. I missed the fight. Shortly thereafter, the United States demolished the Republican Guard in a 100-hour battle. I had missed the fight once again.

On August 26, 1993, I was part of an elite task force of Special Operations Soldiers who deployed to Mogadishu, Somalia to capture an evil warlord. That battle on October 3, 1993 was one of the most intense firefights seen by U.S. troops since the TET Offensive in Vietnam. I was a single, 26-year-old Staff Sergeant with only my men and myself to worry about.

Few people outside of the "community" know the whole story of what would be called Black Hawk Down. While we were deployed for a few months, it was very difficult and emotionally grueling. The carnage from 3 October was immeasurable for many young men who had never seen battle before that day. For me, I was able to return home to my loving parents and siblings. The return home for the wounded and married Soldiers was much different. I am embarrassed that as a young leader I was ill equipped to counsel or help any of my men in other than the most fundamental, though loving way.

For some, the post Somalia experience was painful beyond belief. We had lost comrades in the most brutal way known to man. But, we collectively grieved in our own ways and prepared for the next battle. Many of the Rangers who fought left the Army after their enlistment, and they fell from sight.

In August of 2006, my Company and I deployed from Ft. Drum, New York to Yusufiyah, Iraq in support of Operation Iraqi Freedom. I was now 40 and married with a young daughter at home. This was a much different combat experience for myriad reasons. It was not necessarily a direct action fight; it was a counter insurgency campaign. We would spend fifteen months deployed from home supporting the operation against al-Qaeda as well as the sectarian factions that killed with impunity in ancient Mesopotamia.

Deploying, fighting and returning from Iraq (or Afghanistan) was a much different experience. The thrill of the fight was not as acute, though I supported our effort 100% and then some. This time, I was an infantry Company First Sergeant. I had 120 men and about 60-70 families now under my care. Though I felt confident in my abilities as a manager for the commander, I was still ill equipped to give much in the way of wise counsel for some of my men who were on their third deployment. Three years away from home! I had Soldiers who had spent more time in Baghdad than they had back home in Watertown, New York. What could I possibly do to aid in their re-integration to normalcy?

The short answer is not much. Though I could discuss marriage with the boys based on my own relationship, I had never endured the heartache of separation like the fifteen-month stretch we had to sustain. It's easy, I must say, to "armchair quarterback" the Army and DoD in this process, but that would be grossly unfair. However, a 500,000-man-strong organization can be clumsy and filled with bureaucracy—that's just the way it is. They do the best they can and certainly help many of those who need support.

Shortly after returning from Iraq, I was introduced to Elaine Dumler by a mutual friend. Elaine was effusive in her passion about the Soldiers and their families. She was electric in her heartfelt concern about helping those who need help the most. We spent a long afternoon discussing deployments and combat. I found her to be both engaging and respectful of my privacy, yet easy to talk with. She was determined to make a difference in the lives of so many.

The Road Home is a simple road map for the military family to use before, during and after a tumultuous separation. It fills a gap between a large lumbering system and the personal need for help. Many young families are reluctant to ask for help for a variety of reasons. Elaine provides an opportunity for these most precious men and women to begin their lives back together in peace, harmony, and most of all with love.

We are lucky to have such a gifted woman to answer the call to service. On a memorial wall in Ft. Bragg, North Carolina there is a verse of scripture that reads *and then I heard the voice of the Lord saying who shall I send? And who will go for us? And I said, "Here am I Lord, send me."* Soldiers, Sailors, Airmen and Marines do that when they enlist and agree to serve; Elaine is doing it now.

1SG Matthew P. Eversmann, USA(RET)
Matthew Eversmann was portrayed by Josh Hartnett in the movie "Black Hawk Down."

The Road Home
Your Journey Begins

Why we're here . . .

Welcome to the next step in our journey together. Since 2003, I've been a part of all you've been going through with your military deployments and temporary assignments. The first part of the journey was preparing yourself and your family for deployment. The next part was keeping you strong and connected with each other throughout that deployment or as the case with many of you, multiple deployments. We've become friends. You've shared your families, your hearts, your ideas and stories with me over the years. I saw it as my honor and responsibility to share your ideas with many others in the books *I'm Already Home* and *I'm Already Home...Again*. I've learned so much from you and what you've been going through, and as an active civilian I've become a part of your journey, too. Now we're ready to begin step 3: your journey back home. I say that we're beginning this step because that's what this book is. It's the first look at the joys, challenges and issues involved in bringing you back together.

You've come to expect certain things from me and my books, and I won't let you down. I've helped you while you've been apart, so it only seems logical that I should be a part of helping you come home. As you know, reunion and the entire process of reintegrating is something that takes time. "Home" is a journey, not a destination.

Over the past year, I've begun talking with you to collect your best reunion ideas, stories and resources that were the biggest help to you as you reunited. There have been so many that I often found myself delaying the start of my writing while I waited for all this wonderful information to come in. I can also tell you that this has been a painful process as well. As one woman wrote, "Homecoming is not all balloons and parties!" While bringing people back together is wonderful, many who are returning are not the same people they were when they left. I can't write an honest look at reunion without sharing articles and input from experts on PTSD, combat stress, injuries, and loss. At times, it became a daunting task; one where I felt overwhelmed. I finally realized that I had to begin, and that this book, *The Road Home* is just that . . . a beginning. I'll give you what I have now, knowing that much more will arrive via my website, interviews and phone calls. We'll learn new things, discover new resources and government programs, and I can bring you updated editions over the coming years.

You know that my faith helped me write the first two books, and if I was having trouble getting started with this third one, I considered that maybe I wasn't doing it in God's time. I shared my thoughts with a very special friend, LeAnn. She wrapped me in a comforting hug and said, "If He calls you to it, He'll sustain you through it." It was exactly what I needed to hear. Now I'm ready to begin.

Reunion and reintegration has started to take center stage in the life of a deployment. It's the part that most people look to with joy and anticipation. It's wonderful that you can be together again with a loved one and feel that you can now move your lives forward. Yet even in this relief you find that some significant challenges are creeping in. Some of these are brand new and were never even discussed before the deployment. You know what? That's okay! In fact, just recognizing that it's **not all a bed of roses** is the first step in helping you all get back to normal—whatever that is! You begin to discover that what's happening IS normal—it's just your "new" normal.

My constant piece of advice to you throughout this book is to encourage you to reach out. That means if you think your needs are beyond the scope of this book, please reach out to the support groups, FRG and FAC leaders, chaplains, and some of the myriad resources that are out there to help. We've taken care to compile many of them here for you in the back of this book under **Resources and Support**.

My prayer is for every serviceperson's safe return, and I hope that the messages in *The Road Home* will play a small part in easing your family through the fun and challenging experience of coming together as a family or community again.

That said, welcome to the journey home!

Where we're going . . .

Last year I was speaking for a Navy "Returning Warriors Weekend," and after the general session, I led a smaller workshop addressing some of the concerns people have about returning home after deployments. There were about 60 folks in the room representing both the families at home and the sailors who had just returned. These sessions are usually fun and noisy with all the ideas being tossed out. To begin, I posed the following question to the group, "What is the first thing that comes to your mind when you hear that your spouse is coming home?" A woman about halfway back in the crowd jumped to her feet and without hesitation shouted out, I think, *"How the heck did my butt get this big?!"* Well, those weren't the exact words she used; I toned them down a bit. No matter what the words were, everyone in the room knew exactly what she meant! In fact, one man stood up and said, "My wife is deployed, and when I know she's coming home I look in the mirror thinking that my gut has gotten way out of control." So with this, I'm thinking that it's a "Butts and Guts" kind of thing.

But no matter what *your* first thoughts are, the preparation, excitement and apprehension begin to kick in from the moment you hear the words, "I'm coming home!" Deployment is not just about the time you had apart. Reunion is a vital part of the deployment cycle and it goes beyond the homecoming parties. And single deployments have become multiple deployments. At first, families would "stick it out" thinking that it's only going to be this one time. That's been a rude awakening.

Going through two or three deployments is becoming more and more common.

Even through the unknowns, the families I've met have stepped up to the challenge and continued to work harder and stronger to keep this from taking a permanent toll on their family. What do they say helps them a lot? Being "proactive" instead of "reactive." They know more now about what it's going to be like, and they know where to go for information. They know they have to take charge of their own lives and create the best environment they can for those around them.

We have also discovered that you aren't in this alone. I remember way back in late 2002 and early 2003 when it was determined that family support programs and resources were needed. There wasn't much in play before that time that we knew about. Over the next few years, I watched the development of amazing growth and response in this area as the need continued. The military "answered the call" for the families by establishing programs of support and readiness. The programs grew as the need grew, and it continues today.

The same goes for reunion and reintegration. As our servicemembers began coming home . . . and re-deploying . . . issues were arising in the families and communities. A lot of this stemmed from lack of information and misunderstanding. Once again, I'm seeing the military step up to put help in motion.

Is the system perfect? Far from it, but progress is being made. When this book comes out, the Yellow Ribbon reintegration program will be about six months old, and it resulted from federal legislation. At its very base level, states are required to provide trainings 30, 60, and 90 days following return home. It would be great if circumstances would allow a servicemember to be actively involved in reintegration trainings even a year after his/her return, but that doesn't always happen. At one conference, this issue was brought up: How to track servicemembers in their command after 180 days or so and keep in touch? Some responses included:

- On the unit level, get their cell phone numbers and have a "well" call list just to find out how things are.

- Make better use of "exit interviews." You can record information for follow up.

- Act in a "wingman" concept. No matter the size of the unit, someone out there knows "Joe," where he is and why he left. Take care of each other.

- In each unit, assign someone specific who would be devoted to reunion and reintegration—or at least a contact person. This person could be available to connect people with foundations that provide assistance or other resources.

- Pay special attention to those whose lives take them away, like civilian job transfers, no support system for single servicemembers, and those who have drug/alcohol problems but are not in treatment.

I see the establishment of these programs being rooted in the belief that assistance and resources should be made available on an ongoing basis. I'm proud to be one of those resources.

How we'll get there . . .

Servicepersons don't deploy alone. When they leave they take with them the family members, friends and colleagues who care about them and their well being. More then 57.6 million people are impacted by soldiers, airmen, sailors and marines deployed to Afghanistan and Iraq.[1] When your loved one comes home he or she is also coming home to all those other people. That's why it's important to help everyone affected make this transition as smooth as possible.

The Road Home is designed to help you discover unique and wonderful ways to reconnect and find yourselves again following a deployment or assignment. It's as simple as that. You might already have a couple of traditions in place but would just like to try something new for a change. I hope you find at least a few unique ideas that spark you to think, *That's cool. We should try that.* Take an idea and apply a special twist to it so that your family can own it now.

Throughout the book I refer to soldiers, airmen, sailors and marines as they relate to the origination of a particular idea and who submitted it. Please know that I mean no disrespect when I use these references interchangeably. You're all part of our collective "military family," and most of the ideas are applicable across branch lines.

I encourage you to write on the pages and make personal notes in the margins when something strikes you. Then you'll know where to quickly find that special idea.

Above all, I find that people on both sides of deployment just want an answer to the question, "Am I normal?" Reunion requires change, and change can cause stress as you rediscover what "normal" is. Each chapter of this book will help you answer that question for yourself and most likely you'll find that yes, what you're feeling and experiencing is "normal" and others are feeling it, too. Together we'll look at the blessings and bruises, tears and triumphs, hopes and challenges of your reunion and reintegration and learn what military families around the world are doing and using to smooth the transition back home.

Let me tell you how this book structure came about. As you know by now, over the past years I've spoken with thousands of families about deployments, assignments and reunions. When I knew that it was only a matter of time until I wrote a book about reunion and re-integration, I began to ask people, "What is an area of reunion that you have questions or feel apprehensive about?" As you can imagine, the answers were many and varied, from the wonderfully funny to the very serious. Out of all the responses, many seemed to fall into the nine general categories I've listed below in no particular order:

- Dealing with changed roles at home
- Personal image, sex and intimacy (back together as a couple)
- Getting back into routines with friends and family
- How I'll adjust to my "New Normal"
- Reunion and the kids—especially dealing with discipline
- Fitting back in at work (outside of active service)

- PTSD and combat stress—how to recognize and handle it
- Initial homecoming activities
- How to be sure we are communicating—talking to each other again
- Dealing with loss and grief

Although not in the above "Top 10," the following ideas and thoughts were also expressed:

- Fitting back into the world as a single person and/ or single parent
- Recognizing those who return wounded
- A bit about reuniting "blended" families

I decided that each of the chapters in this book would address one of the above categories where I would share your ideas, resources, stories and solutions as they apply to each. Of course we know that there's a lot more to consider upon reunion, but as I mentioned earlier, addressing these will be our first step.

What military families need to know— Ideas to get us started . . .

As you'd expect, not everything that I want to tell you fits neatly into one of the categories. Unlike a duffle bag, I couldn't cram everything I wanted to say into chapters, and some things just seemed to be over-arching themes that encompassed so much more. There are some general thoughts I want to share as we begin because I liked them!

1 I heard this quite a bit: Be realistic in your expectations of others. This will involve patience on everyone's part, and I know it will take some time, but it's worth it. Someone told me once that if you don't "over expect" a certain response from someone then you won't ever be disappointed. I guess that kind of sums it up, and the reality of what happens will be so much easier to deal with.

My grandparents on my mother's side were married for over 65 years, and from what I saw were very happy. When I was first married, I talked to "Mimi" about what made them get along so well. Her response was short and to the point. She said, "There are two things. First, always sleep in the same bed (they never had twin beds) and never let the sun set on an argument." They could be arguing about something during the day but would always try hard to come to a solution or compatible breaking point before they went to bed. Mimi said that the two pieces of advice went hand-in-hand because it's really hard to sleep in the same bed when you're mad at each other. I know from my own marriage, that's the truth! So to follow on my grandmother's advice, here's what Cheryl said:

2 Remember that if you left a problem on the table when you deployed, it will probably be there when you get back. These concerns just don't disappear—especially when they involve people or money. So what does this mean? Clear up issues before you head out. It's hard to have a disagreement hanging over your heads while you're thousands of miles apart for many months, and who wants it there when you come back?

The next two are ideas that combine what they did during the deployment to stay connected and how it carried over to coming home.

3 "When my husband was deployed to Afghanistan '05—'07, I bought a nice journal and gave it to him. I asked him to write his first letter home in it and mail the book back to us. In return I wrote a letter back to him in it and had our kids do the same, and then I mailed the book back to him. My husband got the idea and kept it up. At the end of the deployment the book was full. All the letters, photos, drawings, poems, news clippings—you name it—were in the book (in order of date written or added). It made us all feel connected in a way that regular mail could not have done. We sent individual letters back and forth, too, and added them to the book later since it took a few weeks to get the book back. We wanted Daddy to get MAIL all the time, not just when we were waiting for the book. He brought it home with him, and the coolest part was looking at it again together when he came home. It makes a wonderful keepsake, and it's something that you can take out anytime and share with others, or just look at it again yourself. It was a great idea and well worth the effort." Thank you so much for sharing that, Irma.

4 Speaking of bringing something home, here's what Nicki did: "I sent him a small jade turtle that he had given me for one of my birthdays. I collect turtles, so he knows it is special to me. I instructed him in my six-page letter to make sure that he returns it to me personally!"

What is something special to you that you can send overseas to be returned personally?

5 Be ready to adapt to change because there will be a lot of it going on. Neither people nor situations will be the same as when you left, even if you were only gone on a short-term assignment. It's important for me to say that as I get to know you better, I see a great deal of resiliency in military families. You put up with a lot, which causes you to stretch out of your comfort zone; when you need to, you can spring back to normal again. It's that resiliency that makes you all so special.

One thing that I heard a number of times in sessions brought by youth and family counselors is to have patience. Please realize that reintegration is not an overnight process, and that's normal! It can take some families up to a year to totally readjust. Not a happy thought, but one that just might help you take everything day by day.

6 Are you a Family Readiness or Family Support leader? Be sure there are systems set up and in place for reintegration issues that families might have so you can be ready to help with the challenges. Know who and what your resources will be when you need them. It's been suggested that you set up your support systems to address the needs in three areas: Short-term immediate needs, moderate needs—those that will begin to show up three to six months after return, and Long-term and ongoing needs. These might involve health and child care, care for wounded, and marriage/counseling assistance.

◆

Personally I find _www.MilitaryOneSource.com_ to be a valuable resource for all three of these areas.

◆

An open letter to the returning servicemember:

Things happened while you were gone, as they had to in order for your home to continue to run itself. Responsibilities changed and sometimes people had to change, too, in order to meet the needs of the household.

The person who remained home discovered that he/she really could balance the checkbook, call in repairmen, do the cooking, get the kids where they had to go and when they had to be there, and make the available money last for the expected length of time. Those successes make people feel good about who they are and what they can accomplish when the need arises; however, feelings of inadequacy may develop if it didn't go as well as planned. Look for positive changes that have occurred, and don't jump on what you perceive as negative changes. Watch for how the changes are working.

You're home now, so everything can return to normal—whatever that is—but probably not right away. There will be a transition period where you'll become "reacquainted" again as a family. If you have small children, don't be alarmed if they cry or resist your hugs immediately. They've been without you for so long, and it takes a while for them to get comfortable with you again. Take time to observe your children in their everyday routines, and slowly allow yourself to become a part of those routines again.

You'll need to reacquaint yourself again with your spouse. Talk about how everything got done at home in your absence. See what worked and what didn't. Maybe things don't have to go right back to the way they were; it might not be the best solution. The key is to share your expectations with each other. Ask your spouse, "Do you want to hand over the checkbook right away, or did you find that you enjoyed that responsibility?" Perhaps he/she would like to continue to be an active part of your family's financial planning. Oh, and don't forget that compliments and expressing appreciation for the extra work he/she did go a long way!

Don't keep all your thoughts secret, but do allow for some "welcome home" time to pass as you bask in the rediscovery of each other. Here's a tip from a family counselor: "Remember that if you maintained closeness and intimacy during the absence, as well as when you're together, then it will feel just like the continuation of what you've been building all along." She also offers, "Love is a decision; decide on romance." We'll talk more about that in the chapter on intimacy. In the meantime, welcome home. We're really glad to have you back!

There is one thought that I want you to keep close throughout this entire time. Everything doesn't happen all at once. You have to continually watch for the little things that happen and cherish the impact that each has on your life. Remember:

Don't expect Miracles; expect Moments!

Chapter One
REUNION - First Days Back

Reunion—First Days Back

◆ ◆ ◆

Everything starts with "The Call" . . .

At first, my logical mind was telling me that reunion begins with your first day back together. Boy did I have that wrong! Preparation begins way before that, at the time you get "the call" that your servicemember is finally coming home. I will start with some general advice from a few people who would like to share what they've learned because they've been through it before. Realize that everyone's experiences with both deployment and reunion are very personal and can be extremely different. My hope in bringing you the thoughts of others is that somewhere, sometime, you'll stumble upon something said that will just "hit home" with you. You'll think to yourself, *Was this person sitting in my kitchen watching us?* I don't want anyone to miss that moment. So pick out what you like best and what you need from the advice given and put it to good use.

I found the most sage advice about where reunion really starts came from Jenn. Her husband is a SSG in the Army. We sat in my office talking about this entire process and her ideas were so good that I just told her to write them down herself so they can come to you directly. Here's what she said:

7 "Weeks before the actual ceremony you will start thinking about all the things you wish you would

have accomplished before he returned. Don't stress yourself out unnecessarily. When your soldier returns he will not notice that you haven't cleaned the tub in weeks or that the carpet needs to be cleaned. He will notice if you are there to greet him. If it is at all possible, meet your spouse at the homecoming ceremony. I have heard from more than one returning soldier how terrible it was to arrive there and see everyone else be greeted by loved ones. So focus on what is really important.

Also, stay flexible. Your FRG or FAC's really will do the best job they can communicating to you when the ship or boat is returning or when your soldier or marine will land at the airfield. However, as with anything in the military the only constant is change. Stay flexible and "keep your eye on the prize" so to speak. Ultimately, your soldier will return home when the military says so. Try to be ready when the call comes. Often times change occurs at the last minute, so plan to arrive early just in case!

8 In preparation for the homecoming ceremony, do take care of the things that have been neglected, but consider that messy yard your "gift" to him . . . "I know how you love yard work, Honey, so I saved it for you." It's been said that the state of the yard is directly correlated to the length and number of deployments, and I think it has to be true. When you are the "spread thin 'single' parent" you prioritize, and somehow pulling weeds never made it to the top of my list until the HOA (Homeowners Association) told me I had to. Neither did changing light bulbs.

9 Communicate with your ombudsman or FRG leader. They will be a direct link to those who are in the know. They are hopefully doing a good job keeping

you informed as they get updates, but don't be afraid to call and ask or send an email to your FRG leader or FAC if you have questions. Those last few weeks or days before the ceremony were crazy at my house. My own To Do List went right out the window because there were so many "inquiring minds," and that was okay. Ultimately when Mike came home, he didn't care about all the things I hadn't had a chance to finish. But he did appreciate being home and sleeping in clean sheets in his own bed and that first home-cooked meal.

10 Attend any demobilization or reunion info sessions you can. Even if you hate your FRG, and we know some of you do, there will be information presented that will be valuable to you. Once your soldier gets here, you might not want anything to do with the military. TRUST ME, that might be the case for at least a few weeks, perhaps even months. So now before your world turns upside down with his return, attend these meetings and make sure your name and information is updated to get last-minute phone calls and emails about homecoming changes. There will be important details distributed by people who know things that you don't even know you need to know!

Everyone else you know will start asking when he is coming home weeks before he actually does. And they will all say, "Wow, ___weeks; that is really getting close." Resist the urge to scream! However many weeks is short compared to what you've endured, but it will still drag by at moments. In hindsight, it will seem to have flown by! In those moments of inquiring minds, be careful what info you release. Unfortunately in today's world, we do need to be cognizant of operational security. For the safety of your soldier or sailor, limit the details you divulge. Unless they are a family member planning to attend the ceremonies, they do not need to know exact times, dates and locations. Of course, you can probably trust your friends, but you never know who else is listening when you are having a conversation, so use caution just in case.

As you prepare for the return, know that all your feelings really are normal. All those doubts, questions and worries are being had by other loved ones in your battalion, and so rest assured someone has been there. I by no means mean to trivialize what each individual is going through, but older, wiser, experienced friends or FACs can be a great resource.

All those *Will he still love me? Will he be different? Will I still like him?* thoughts are normal. In no time at all you will have one of those *Ahhh, I forgot you do that* thoughts about some annoying habit you romanticized in his absence. It will all come back to you quickly enough. So enjoy for now.

Even happy change is stressful. Be flexible, be patient, and communicate with each other and those who know something you may not.

I promise there is nothing else like the energy you will feel in that gymnasium, hangar or airfield as the guys deplane or disembark or even just march through the door. The first time you lay eyes on him again will be a moment and a feeling that you will never forget. It's overwhelming being surrounded by a crowd of strangers or even friends who feel the same way about seeing their own servicemember for the first time in weeks, months or even years. You will feel a connection to those people, even though the moment is an intimate one.

11 Be prepared for your kids to feel a sense of being emotionally overwhelmed, as well. I did not expect my kids to be so emotional. They are boys and they rarely show emotion, but we all sobbed that day. Of course, they were tears of joy at his safe return, but nonetheless it was emotionally draining.

12 If possible, do make friends with others who are going through it. Your sister and friends from your hometown are great, but having someone who is feeling it while you are is a great comfort. I could not have survived without my battle buddies, and through my FRG involvement I met quite a few.

13 Also, if possible bring a personal photographer to the ceremony. If it is someone who knows you but doesn't feel the need to participate in the hugging, great! Count yourself lucky! That will allow you to focus and so can he, without extra people to hug and kiss. Having those photos to look back on will be something you cherish. My friend Deb took pictures for us and I am so glad she did. She had never met Mike, so there was no expectation or sense of obligation for either of them. He did hug her hello after our moment was finished, but he didn't even know she was "with us" until the excitement settled down and I introduced them.

Overall, try to limit the extra people who attend. There will be a time and place where your hubby can greet his neighbors, your best friend from college, and his football buddies, but here in this homecoming moment, less really is more. Mike was so appreciative that it was just the kids and me in that moment. Weeks before he told me his ideal homecoming would be just the boys and me in an empty room. Well, the event center wasn't empty, but everyone else there was enjoying their own intimate reunion moment so it was the next best thing. No one else was standing there waiting to hug him, so he could and did focus on each of us individually and as a group.

14 Prep your kids for the things you know. "Dad will be less patient than you remember," or "We need to give Dad some space." It will be tempting not to let him out of your sight for the first few days, and most units do a good job forcing you to by requiring demobs and refits. You may need to reassure your kiddos that he will go to work . . . "but just until lunch time," or "Dad needs a little break." I also tried to get my kids to understand that Dad really missed us. He had only his battle buddies and coworkers, and he was in a strange place with no one who loved him. We at least had each other this whole time, our house, our dog, our friends, our schools, all the people we normally saw. Sure our routines had been a little different, but we got to sleep in our own beds and celebrate our holidays at home. We missed him and only him, while he had to miss everyone. That really helped my kids.

15 In the first weeks back, I made sure to spend alone time with my kids without their dad. They were used to having my attention and talking to me about their feelings, and those first few weeks were stressful. The first time Mike snapped at one of the kids, I felt the need to "circle the wagons" and protect my kiddos, even though I love my husband. Make time to pull kids aside or at least be open to moments of conversation where they can release what they are feeling about Dad being back. I found that driving somewhere with the two of them worked great. Just me and my boys. We could have a conversation where no one was forced to make eye contact—the rear view mirror is not as intimidating as Mom staring you down, and we could really talk about it. It was a natural opportunity, not forced; it worked great for us.

A few different times Grant said, "Dad sure is grumpy," when we all came down off of the adrenaline high of homecoming. I tried to get him to see and understand that Dad had even more changes to adjust to than we did. At ten, he really was able to understand that. He's a little sponge and implements the things he hears easily without much effort. That helped him to realize he needed to be mindful of his behavior and not try Dad's patience more than necessary. Of course, he was still a kid, and I circled the wagons a few times in those first couple of months. I did run interference for them, acting as a buffer sometimes to make it go more smoothly for everyone involved. Mike didn't want to feel like he was yelling or getting impatient either. So I did feel a sense of responsibility to make sure everyone had all their cards on the table, so to speak. And the kids knew what was expected.

16 Immediately after the return home, if you can avoid it, don't force anything to change such as discipline, haircuts, budgeting, etc. Rash decisions can be made in the days that follow that "reunion honeymoon," but those changes are sometimes irreversible. Kids are stressed, too, about how Dad will feel about them, so accept what you can. Mike had to endure a "hippie" haircut on Grant for a bit. When he couldn't take it anymore he forced Grant to get his haircut, and boy was Dad sorry. The barber didn't listen, and Grant ended up "scalped." Dad realized that having his kid feel like he hadn't "fit his mold" made Grant feel terrible. Mike will never force a haircut again, and even though I know Grant has forgiven it, he will never forget "the time Dad made the barber shave his head." More importantly, he will remember how that made him feel.

17 **Driving:** Most units will caution service-members not to drive for a little while post deployment. This is for many reasons, so take it slow. Many freshly returned servicemembers commit traffic violations and are issued tickets in the first few days back. The "deployment" card doesn't usually work in these instances. They may need some time to adjust back to our traffic rules. If they've been driving with no speed limit in which every lane is empty, even the oncoming one, they may still instinctually try to do that once they return. Allow some time before driving is expected or even allowed.

How's that for jumping right in with some great overall advice? Thanks to Jenn and her family for letting us take a look into that critical prep time.

Now let's hear from Ashley. What I like especially about her advice is that even though it's written with her spouse in mind, I found it to be good advice for all family members of a serviceperson. I've taken the liberty of substituting "servicemember" for "spouse" so that you'll all identify with what she shares.

"We have had many deployments and many homecomings over the last seven years. Before your servicemember leaves overseas, you might be talking about big plans for when he/she comes home. You want this time to be special, so you might be thinking about a vacation or having lots of things planned to make this time special, but one that would throw him/her face first into the world that was missed. I caution you, for their sake and yours, this might not be the reality you experience when he/she gets home. Many times we make plans to do special things, to go here or there when we're together again. So . . .

18 Try as hard as you can not to get hurt when only some (or even none) of those plans really happen. The reality is that he or she will be soooo very tired from jet lag and will have just traveled several days to get back to you here at home. He/she will be tired. The truth is, after the welcome home celebration he/she will want to SLEEP.

Of course it's normal to be offended that sleep is taking priority, but try to cut a little slack. For the past year, your servicemember has been on a very different time schedule from yours. It takes time to adjust. Be patient. He/she really does want to do all those things you have planned, but for right now is happy with just sitting on the couch watching TV or doing things around the house. Remember that when your servicemember gets home, those plans you made will not be as important to your loved one as just being there in the same house with you."

19 Here's something that Ashley did to let the others in her husband's unit know that they are all part of the same military family. "I made three slideshows while my husband was gone. The first and third were for our own family, and the second is a tribute to him and his fellow coworkers. Throughout the deployment he sent me pictures of everyone, and I used these in their slideshow. I wanted to pay tribute to all of them for their time and sacrifice and tell them that all they went through was not forgotten or overlooked. I am proud of each and every one of them. This was THEIR TRIBUTE! If it weren't for them risking their lives, we wouldn't have the freedom we enjoy. I made copies of the slideshow and sent them to the people who were in the photos. This was sent in support of the red, white and blue!"

You know the best part? Ashley sent me the slideshows she made so that I got to see them, too. They were wonderful, and Ashley says that they weren't all that difficult to produce.

20 Jean's advice starts at home. She suggests that you "only make minor decorative changes to the house (who cares if it's clean or not), indulge in primping yourself so you look and feel your best, get the kids to design *Welcome Home* tee shirts with fabric paint, and then go to the MOB site and wait. After all it's one of the best days of your life!"

James agrees. He says to go easy on the decorating and rearranging. He and many others really want the comfort and familiarity of coming home to exactly the surroundings they left. It lends a great sense of security. In fact, he said, "After the Gulf War, I wish my wife had labeled items around the house! I felt like I was in someone else's home, not mine. I had to ask where the towels and soap were and things like which cabinet the canned goods were in now." He may have said this with a bit of jest, but in reality, "It was weird not to know where things were."

Our next pieces of sage wisdom are from two women who are in dual service marriages. I guess that gives them twice the insight. Our first, Angela, says that "Reunion and reintegration for our family presents new challenges each time we go through it. The things that worked best for us were:

21 Have few expectations and be very patient with one another.

22 Another helpful thing was to blank out time on the calendar. We limited visitors to very select people and did not plan to travel or vacation right off. We took things very slowly while getting to know each other again and fitting back into one another's routines."

Melanie says, "My husband deployed to Iraq in 2004. We both serve in the military so it was easier for me to understand what he was going through. Even being in the military I found myself losing patience with not knowing what was going on, when they were leaving, when they were getting to their FOB, when he was coming home for R&R, etc. The most difficult was when he was returning for good.

23 The best advice I can give is to remember that everyone is different in what they envision for their reunion. Communication is essential. I envisioned a romantic dinner that night with no kids and a night on the town. He envisioned going to bed to sleep and unwind and then some 'cuddle' time. Like I said, communication is essential! If I had gone ahead and made my plans without talking with him, we'd both have been miserable.

24 I also remember that my first reaction was to meet him at his MOB site when he first returned. From our experience, this wouldn't have worked. He was exhausted from his long trip. He had several long days ahead of him to complete everything he needed to get done in order to be done for good. Those few days allowed him to get readjusted and catch his breath.

(**Author's note:** I have now presented both sides of this issue, so be sure to evaluate your personal circumstances and do what's best for **your** family and not for others.)

So for me, the two major keys I found to a successful reunion were communication (as much as possible) and patience! I wish you all a safe deployment and a wonderful reunion. God Bless!"

You remember Melanie saying that you really do need to communicate about what your homecoming plans are. Most families are just fine showing up at the airport and continuing home to a planned event that you all are expecting. Not sure exactly what to do to make this event even more special? Let's hear what others have done.

Touchdown!—Love at first sight . . .

The schedule for returning starts on the tarmac and that first ride home. It seems like a good place to start with the next four contributions.

25 When meeting your serviceperson, have a really large poster board with his/her name on it so it can be spotted easily—because the Troops "all look alike in uniform!" Decorate the poster with your own flair.

26 Have the unit create a Welcome Home banner with ALL the soldiers' names on it, and make another one with the names of the fallen soldiers. This is a recognition that often passes us by at the return home. These posters can be hung permanently in the armory or on base.

Speaking of banners, how about these!

27 "When my husband came home on leave I had Steamroller Copies® make me a "Welcome Home—We Love You" banner in patriotic lettering. I colored it red, white and blue. Then I hung it up for him to see when he came home. It cost me a whole $2.50! Well, instead of throwing it away, I decided that I was going to let everyone who knows my husband and me write a little message to him on the banner. I will be putting our son's handprints on it, too. That way, when we go to pick him up at this current homecoming, he will be able to see how many people missed him while he was gone. I will also be taking pictures of the people signing it for a memories book. This is something simple yet fun, and something that will be truly enjoyed forever." – Amber

28 "At the local print shop on base, my kids and I made a welcome home poster for my husband. We were able to use this at the airport, for his Welcome Home open house with friends and family, and for his first days back at church, work, etc. It wasn't expensive, and they were able to design it exactly how we wanted— as a large poster we could roll up and keep. My kids were into specific video games, clubs and such so they included clipart from those games on the poster. Everyone loved the idea of it, and it sort of told the 'story' of what we all did while Dad was deployed. The gist of it, of course, read *Welcome Home Chris/Dad*, and we used the clipart and photos to show how we spent the time while he was gone. This was about seven years ago, and he still has it!

For those who don't want someone else to create it, it can be created on a home computer, or you could buy your own poster board and hand make the sign. Be sure to make it 'thematic' so it can be read and enjoyed as something personal. Some of the things to graphically display on it can be:

- what the spouse and kids did while the parent was deployed;
- what we love about Dad/Mom;
- what we'll do now that he/she is home; and so on.

We worked on this poster probably two months prior to him arriving home. That gave us plenty of time to make changes and decide on other things we wanted to add.

It was a great interactive project to do with the children while we were waiting. The print shop was able to email it to us so we could print out copies to use as placemats at home or prints to share with family. And we'll always have the file in case the original gets damaged." – Lisa

29 This is called "Every Step You Take, I'll be Watching You." Find places to post signs along your loved one's route from the airport (or base) to home. Some examples of signs to make and hang are:

> 30 miles to love
> 20 miles to home cooking
> 10 miles to the remote
> 2 miles to hugs

You'll think of some great ones.

30 "Our soldiers came home midday and the local Chamber of Commerce got all the businesses lining the route rallied up for a celebration. There were thousands of people lining the streets and waving flags, welcoming our soldiers home. The soldiers were so overwhelmed they cried, as did the families riding in the convoy." – Deidre

31 When pulling in the driveway, he will see 100 yellow ribbons tied to the trees in front of the house, and perhaps he'll hear the yellow ribbon song, too!

32 Talk about making a sign that really hits a person with what he/she likes, this one was genius: "When my brother pulled into the driveway after his deployment, he saw a huge banner on the garage door that read **'Guinness served here!'** Then he knew he had to be home!"

33 Another great idea: "Dad was TDY for school in Alaska for one year. We became very used to being without him, and when he came home, the first night was weird! So Mom came up with the idea of PJs, popcorn, and a kid movie all bunched up under one blanket. We needed to touch him, to know it was real; then everyone relaxed."

Remember when families made "TDY Countdown Jars" to tick off the time until the serviceperson returns home? Below I'm sharing a reminder of that idea (just in case you're not familiar with it) because what she did with the jars after he returned was really cool and was something I had never thought of before.

34 "TDY Countdown Jars can be made out of any type of container, decorated by the child/ children with supervision. Fill each jar with individual candies, fruit snacks, Flintstone vitamins, etc. The parent counts out the number of pieces to put in the jar according to the number of days the other parent is deployed. Once each day, a piece is removed from the jar. When the jar is empty, Daddy/Mommy (brother/ sister/son/daughter) is home. The parent at home can add or take away from the jar according to days extended or for early release. This is pretty much a work in progress. Pick a specific time of day for the child to take one from the jar. You can even add fill lines: Full, ¾, ½, nearly there, home!

Scrap bookers can go crazy with the designs for these jars for those too young to put it together themselves, or help toddlers with their creativity. My children loved this idea! They looked forward to their treat each day, knowing it would bring Dad home sooner (in their eyes).

I did have to add about fifteen extra treats, but I made sure to do it while they were sleeping, and gradually, so they wouldn't notice. Each base we've been to, I've been able to pass this idea on and the kids and parents alike love it.

My husband is currently in Iraq on another deployment. Though my children are teenagers now, they still love it, and so do I. I now make one for me, too! Why should the kids have all the fun? For his homecoming, we will decorate the house using the now empty jars for decorative candles (with liners) until the next time they are needed again!" – Lisa

Celebrate!—Right now it IS all about balloons and parties . . .

Ready for the next step? Sounds like there might be a homecoming party in the works. But first, it's important not to go overboard immediately. Many families tell me that it's really hard to hold back. The first key is to discuss the plans you're considering for homecoming with the person who will be returning. Ask them what they have in mind, if anything. Do they want a party right away, or would they rather have a week or so to unwind and then have a party? You'll want to know this. This holds true for all absences and returns, no matter the length or purpose. At the very least, it's the courteous thing to do, and this communication can avoid a disruption of how you envisioned the activities. Communication! Communication! Communication! Here's what some families have done:

35 "We had a small welcome home with just my returning wife, me and the kids. I actually made a great dinner and just let her sit back and enjoy. Then we waited about two or three weeks and had a big outside barbeque with our parents and friends. She was so grateful that she didn't have to have lots of people around right away." Something to consider.

36 "We called our welcome home party *My Favorite Things*. They were all there, all his favorite things that he missed while gone like: favorite foods, favorite dessert, decorations in favorite colors, favorite pictures, a video of events, and of course favorite friends. While everyone was together, we showed the video our family made. We called it *Video of the Year Missed*."

37 "My husband was gone on assignment for six months, and when he got back we included everyone in a welcome back block party in the neighborhood. It was easier to invite people to a party like that, and I had lots of help from the neighbors preparing things like salads. We set up grills in the street, and it was really informal. Then my husband could feel free to 'hang back' and reconnect as he wanted to."

38 Renee reminds us to "be flexible and avoid tight schedules that put too many demands on servicemembers' time at the beginning."

39 Here's something fun. "We used *Time* Magazine's Person of the Year cover (the one that honors the American Serviceperson from December 29, 2003) and placed my daughter's face on the face of one of the soldiers and screened it onto t-shirts for the entire family." (**Author's note:** to see that original cover go to www.time.com/time/covers and search for "Person of the Year.")

40 One mom kept a copy of all the emails, with the replies, that were exchanged with her son during his assignment. She printed them all, three-hole punched them, and put together a notebook. When he returned, she gave him this notebook at the homecoming party. Afterwards, as he was readjusting, he loved rereading these because it let him remember all that he had done on assignment to help others. You tend to forget the impact you can have.

40 My office assistant, Jenn, said that her husband loves "Bomb Pop®" popsicles so when her husband returned home, she cleared everything out of the freezer and filled it to the top with Bomb Pops®! So what's your loved one's favorite treat? Go ahead and go overboard with it.

Three closing thoughts:

42 As a Family Assistance Center Specialist, the one thing that I hear often from the soldiers themselves is, "I wish that when I came home my loved one would not have planned such a large homecoming at the house." The soldier really wants to come in the home and share this time with just his/her immediate family. It was suggested to wait for a couple of weeks to have the big Welcome Home party. I understand this, and I know they are trying to resume a family relationship as well as learning not to be with their *other* family—the soldiers with whom they were deployed. The transition can be very stressful. Everyone needs patience, understanding, and most of all communication with their loved one before the soldier comes home, as well as after they are home." – Linda

Hmmm...communication. How many times have we heard this before? It's turning out to be the basic foundation on which much of what we talk about will be built. This goes right along with what Brenda has to share:

43 "Take the time to be a family again. Shut the rest of the world out for a little while."

44 Are you one of the more than 8,000 families who had a Flat Daddy® or Flat Mommy made as a family "bookmark" while your loved one was gone? As you know this is something that has been a cornerstone of what I believe in and is very close to my heart. (See Idea #179 for more detail about Flat Daddy®.) The question may arise of what to do with him/her now that your real Daddy or Mommy is home. Here's what a number of families have done and I love it. On the first night back, when the parties are over and it's you and your wonderful family, have one more ceremony. Together you can relegate Flat Daddy® to the closet now that real Daddy or Mommy is here to take over. Your Flat Daddy® has been extremely vigilant in watching over the family and now it's time for him to have a break. Let's hope he never has to come out of the closet again!

Now move forward from here and get back to enjoying being back together again—as a family and as a community.

Chapter 2
REINTEGRATION – Life Moves Forward

Reintegration—
Life Moves Forward

◆ ◆ ◆

Adjusting to your NEW "Normal" . . .

Through all the interviews I conducted in the research phase of this book, I found that generally, service-members and families just want to know that what they're feeling and experiencing is somewhat normal and that they're OK. Even if it's shaky at first, it helps to know that things will calm down, and more than likely you'll find that others have been sharing the same concerns that you have. It's amazing how much better that can make you feel. If you had a good relationship with those around you before you left, and you worked to stay connected while you were apart, then the majority of you will blend back into your lives after a while when you get back. I love it when I hear someone say, "I knew we'd have some issues, but I also knew we'd be alright."

A few people shared their thoughts on what it took to help each other make adjustments. If someone else can share what they discovered over time, it just might help you find the answers right now. That's how I feel when I read what Rachael submitted:

45 "When my husband returned home it was an immediate relief, but now, almost five years later, we still find times when we don't really connect. I spent too much time telling him that there was something wrong with him, and not enough time trying to accept the "New Normal." We watch Oprah or Dr. Phil, and they give great advice, but be careful not to turn around and diagnose your soldier. We are not the experts, but we are the avenue to the experts and resources to help. Talk to your unit support or your reintegration office, and tell them what you are experiencing. They can help incorporate that into the returning home reintegration process without the soldier ever knowing who offered the suggestions. Don't try to create the 'cure,' instead accept the new normal."

Here are a few other suggestions people had:

46 "Take a long-term approach to reintegration. Things might be rocky in the short-term, but over time your family life will be normal again. Go slowly and take it one day at a time. Just hang in there."

47 Remember that both parties should be open to change. You both have to compromise. Boy, can that be hard to do. I found that it takes great personal control to "give up" some of your position in order to find your way closer to the middle.

48 This last one is like being protective body armor for the other person. The woman who offered this said that she tries to help protect him from others' judging him on what he is going through. She says acting as that "armor" also helps her really feel the love and support she has for him everyday.

From canteen to watercooler—
Fitting back in on the job . . .

Not only are you coming back to a family you've been away from for so long, but also your "family" at work. You spent eight to ten hours a day with these people and they felt the loss of your presence. You'll actually find that many of the things you do to fit back in at home will work here, too—like communication, patience and tolerance. The good news is that this transition usually isn't as difficult as you might have expected. Yes, things do go on, as does the work needed to get done, but I'll bet that they're glad to have you back. Here are some ideas that have come in on how to make this a smooth transition for everyone:

49 An FRG lead volunteer suggested that they host a community/military "job fair." This can be done on the unit or state level. You can extend it to include civilians and actually have the recruiting booths set up to share what job opportunities the military offers, too. When you think of a job fair, usually it's assumed that it's set up only to help those individuals who are looking for work. Not necessarily. While that could be your focus, have people from different companies offer seminars or workshops on general applicable topics like fitting back into the workplace, working with HR departments, communication between employees and employers, and identifying what your workplace benefits are. Then it becomes informational in nature, too.

50 If you're coming back to a job that might not fit your needs anymore, you can take advantage of the timing to maybe start looking for a new job that better fits your skills and expectations. This seems like a natural break point.

**If you discover that your employer was particularly great in your absence, and you are not active duty,
consider nominating them for an ESGR
(Employer Support of Guard and Reserves)
Patriot Award.
Go to *http://www.esgr.org/forms.asp?p=patriot*
for more information.**

---

51 To those who work around you, you're a hero who's been to a part of the world (if you were a part of the Global War on Terror) or country (if you were on domestic disaster relief) they most likely won't see. They're naturally interested in some of what you did and what that area was like. One way to help them feel involved is to bring them back small, appropriate gifts that were native to that area. Local handcrafted items seem to make good presents. As one woman put it, "Bring lots of gifts for coworkers!" These gifts can also serve another purpose. They are small tokens to show your appreciation to your coworkers and your boss for picking up the slack where necessary while you weren't there.

Through many conversations with employers and returning servicemembers alike, I found a number of tips that I really liked and found easy to do. They were the ones that people said made the biggest difference in how someone was able to fit back in. See what works for you and for the specifics of your job.

Two suggestions for while you're gone, or shortly before you are heading back:

52 Keep connected with at least one coworker during deployment. This will most likely be through email. Have him or her keep you filled in on what's new and what's happening in the workplace. Then the changes won't be such a surprise when you're in the midst of things again. It can show your continued interest in your place of work.

53 Jenn suggested that the spouse at home have the deployed person's coworkers' information, too. It helped Jenn feel she could keep them "filled in" on how her husband was doing and provided another base of support. It goes one step further in helping the company feel connected to those deployed.

54 Along with keeping in touch with a coworker, also keep in touch with your boss or manager. This contact most likely won't be as often as with the coworker, but your boss will have information relevant to your position that you'll want to know and keep up on. Definitely email your boss about setting up a time to talk as soon as you are back from deployment. They graciously maintained your job even though it was federally protected. This should be one of the first things you do to get back up to speed with your civilian career.

It's good to be back on the job, but don't expect it to be exactly as you left it. Things had to move forward—

much like they did at home. There will be new people and new projects. Now you have to find ways to make it all work. As you look at the submitted ideas below, it can seem like all the effort is coming from your end! You're right. Initially, you're the "newbie" in their environment, and cautious consideration on your part is really the best way to let others around you see how it's all going to work. Let's start with:

55 Be willing to adapt to changes that have occurred in the workplace. It may not even look the same as when you left, and some of the people may have changed. Certainly projects that you worked on have since been completed and new ones begun. Don't feel defensive and think, *This isn't the same place I left*, because you're not the same person returning, either. Let people tell you about the changes and how they participated in them. Work hard to accept the changes and not have it be "my way or the highway."

56 Know that it will take time to get readjusted. Don't expect too much, too soon. You might even "stand back" a bit and observe. Watch how people are interacting with each other and take this time to familiarize yourself with what's going on. Then at the first staff meeting you'll actually know the names of the people who are new to you!

57 If someone had to take over your job to keep it up and running while you were unable to, then meet one-on-one with them immediately. How can you best make the transition back without making the person feel unneeded anymore? Again, it's exactly like returning home and immediately trying to take over all the finances from your spouse who did a great job with them in your absence. Be sensitive to how they are feeling about you being back. Take it slowly, and be sure you tell them what a good job they did (if it's true, of course) and how much you appreciate what they did so that you could step back in again.

58 Be extra willing to get along with old and new workers. You might even find that you have to relearn or retrain for parts of your job to keep up with the technologies and procedures that may have changed. Know that sometimes people who have "held down the fort" could be a little resentful that you can come right back to the job you left. Understand that that's natural, and please just be aware.

59 Stay confident in the fact that you did a great job before, and you'll do a great job again! At first you may find that you have to spend a little more time "catching up" and be willing to take that time. It will be easier than you thought with a little care on your part. Just do what you would want others to do if the roles were reversed. (Always a good idea.)

60 If you still have specific concerns about the job, people, or just fitting in, set an appointment to meet personally with your employer. Often it can be more comfortable to meet in a more informal environment like going out to lunch. In turn, this makes your employer feel that you care enough to see that this transition will work well for everyone.

61 If, after you've done all you can, you still feel a bit alienated and uncomfortable, try to think back to the roots of why you took this job in the first place. You had good reasons and you liked it once. They may be different now, but there are core reasons for why you'd really want to make this work and get back to enjoying your job. In a marriage, if you start to see a level of unease or complacency kick in, counselors tell you to remember what first attracted you to each other. You can do the same for a job because it's a big part of your life, and we know that if you're happy in your work, it spills over into your family.

Finally, if you're returning to work with any level of PTSD (Post Traumatic Stress Disorder) or TBI (Traumatic Brain Injury), it may be even harder for people to know how to react to you and understand what you're going through, no matter how much they would like to. Here is a resource that was forwarded to me that might help the employer, employee and coworkers. Often it just takes a little compassion!

---◆---

http://AmericasHerosAtWork.gov
**has a mission statement that says
"helping transitioning veterans
succeed in the work place."
This site provides information for employers
about TBI and PTSD as well as guidance
on implementing workplace accommodations
for affected employees.
They also supply job coaching
and mentoring programs.**

---◆---

Budget is not a dirty word— Avoiding financial pitfalls . . .

It's never been a surprise that sex and money are the two biggest things that can cause relationships to crumble. We'll talk about sex in a later chapter. So for now, let's talk about money. I put this piece near the beginning because it's a part of reintegration that needs to be dealt with as it arises. You can't afford to wait.

Finances changed while you were apart, from the amount of money you actually were able to deposit, to how that money was handled and by whom. Fighting over money is not fun, so let's see if we can look at some financial guidelines to help you stay on the right track no matter what your situation. To help with this, I again went to those who are "in the know."

Some tips on avoiding the most common financial pitfalls upon reintegration by *Crystal Strain, Family Program Specialist, Colorado National Guard Foundation.* Crystal is married to Pete who is in the Air Guard and they have two children.

Most servicemembers and their families fall into three main categories upon deployment, and of course the return home can bring about changes in the finances as well. Each category and family is unique in their circumstances. The following describes the basic three categories most servicemembers will find themselves in.

1. **Stable:** Servicemembers who see a minor increase in pay as they are in an active status with their "day job during the week."

2. **Increase:** Servicemembers who see a major increase in pay when they are activated from a Guard or Reservist status.

3. **Decrease:** Servicemembers who see a decline in pay as their military pay is less than their civilian status pay. A spouse who must cut back on the number of hours she/he works or childcare expenses rise.

In the first category servicemembers see very little change in their income, with some exceptions such as the family separation pay and hazardous duty pay. Your income will pretty much stay the same, as well as your expenses during the deployment.

The biggest pitfall you are likely to run into is the "treat syndrome."

"We have been through so much this deployment. I want to buy my wife/husband something to show her/him how much I love and missed her/him."

"The kids had a hard time but they were amazing so now I want to treat them."

"I deserve to do something nice for myself since I was in the 'sandbox.'"

"Because I was alone and did everything by myself while she/he was gone I want . . . ."

The solutions to the "treat syndrome" are:

1. Put into savings some "fun" money so you can afford to treat yourself and the family to either individual gifts or even a family gift such as a trip the whole family will enjoy.

2. Instead of items to be given to your family, understand that they really want to just spend time with you as the one who has returned. They do not want to share you with the "world." Try to make time with just your immediate family, and then one-on-one with each member.

The second category for servicemembers is where they see an increase in their pay during the training and deployment phase. They are typically enlisted Guard or Reservists and they earn more with their military status than in their civilian status.

The pitfall to watch out for is higher living standards:

You may become adjusted to living above your "normal" means of living. The training and deployment will end, and you will return to your normal standard of income and expenses. Once this happens and the bills continue to come in but your civilian pay does not match your military pay, your stress levels rise!

The following are some solutions to this pitfall:

1. Budget! Budgeting is not a dirty word; it is simply a means to a greater goal that your family may have. But plan on allowing some extra wiggle room in your budget during the deployment.

2. Automatically have the extra income go into a savings account. At the end of your deployment

you very well could have the funds to go on a trip together, or have a down payment for a home or a new vehicle.

3. Even if you decide to keep things simple upon your return, just allow the funds to sit in your savings account. You will be growing it with interest and giving your family a cushion to fall back on should things go wrong!

4. Have an understanding between both husband and wife. Nothing gets added into the budget without both agreeing the new item can be sustained on the pre-deployment budget.

The third category is the family that sees a decline in income due to the deployment. This category has many potential scenarios. The servicemember may have a side business or perhaps in a civilian status his/her income was more substantial. Maybe the spouse has had to cut back on hours or take a leave of absence altogether. Or maybe your childcare expenses have gone up.

The pitfalls for this category can be many and hard to plan for. But planning is exactly what will help you succeed!

The solutions will need to be tweaked to fit your family, and planning is critical.

1. Look for ways to trim your monthly expenses.

2. Try to swap childcare with friends or family. Don't worry about using your friends to help you get through this time because they want to help you and your family. Let them!

3. If you have advance notice of your deployment, build up your savings account prior to your leaving to lessen the sting. Know exactly what the difference will be with your income.

There are some other general guidelines to help you and your family stay above the pitfalls that are out there to trip up your short- and long-term goals:

- Stay away from payday loan places. The benefit is short-lived as your interest rate at these places will never allow you to get ahead or even make ends meet.

- It is important for both the servicemember and their spouse to be on the same page for your life together. Finances can be a button pusher in most relationships. Come up with your family's budget together. If you both are not on board then it is such a struggle. Don't be afraid to let your kids know what your goals are. If you can explain to them the reason you are or are not doing something and what you hope the result will be, it will help them to feel more a part of the family's inner workings and perhaps not give you as much grief!

- Enjoy each other and realize mistakes will happen with your finances. What is important is to get back on track, don't blame each other, and work together!

With the ups and downs of our economy, many people rely too heavily on the instant gratification that credit cards can offer. Others use credit cards for expenses that are larger than they would normally be able to pay off. I found the following checklist in part of an Air Force

Family Support Center booklet, and I thought it was right on.

Are you headed for credit card trouble?

Check each statement that is true about you. Two or more checks could mean trouble.

☐ You hide your monthly credit card statements, or the things you buy, so your family won't discover them.

☐ More than 20% of your take-home pay is used to pay credit cards.

☐ You delay paying other bills so you can pay your credit cards.

☐ You usually pay only the minimum monthly payments.

☐ You charge more each month than you make in payments.

☐ You've used the cash advance on one credit card to make payments on other credit cards.

☐ You've seriously considered a consolidation loan to pay off your credit cards.

☐ You've received a phone call about a delinquent account.

☐ You don't know how much you owe within $500.

☐ The balance on your savings account is shrinking.

☐ You borrow from friends or relatives to make ends meet.

☐ Life would be almost impossible if you lost all your credit cards.

If you think you could use some help, please contact a personal finance program manager or find someone at MilitaryOneSource.com.

From barracks to backyard— Getting back into routines with friends and family . . .

This is such a general category, and I found that many of the ideas are "flushed out" in other chapters. Most people can pretty much just pick up and move forward with family and friends, although there is an adjustment period where they are getting to know each other again. What follows are things that people told me they did to help with that reconnection period of time. You just might find something here that will work for you, too, and a few things that just sound fun!

62 First, I heard people say that they put together a brief action plan for reconnecting so that everyone was in it together and knew the steps they were going to take. They felt that this made the time more purposeful and real and less "spur of the moment." Also, when there was a plan, it made everyone feel they had a part in what was going on.

63 "What worked for our family was to keep lines of communication open. I know we say this over and over, but maybe there's a reason for that. We made it a point to feel free to 'talk, look and renegotiate.' This means that when there were times we disagreed (and there were many at the beginning) we'd step back, take an honest look at what was happening, and be willing to look at things from a different perspective. Boy does this take lots of patience!" – Thanks, Carol

64 Remember that personal time helps everyone get along better too. Just because you're back together, doesn't mean that you have to spend every moment together. You did things on your own during the deployment, and you'll feel deprived if you don't have time to keep those activities going. What hobby do you like? Is it important for you to get off by yourself and read? If that's part of who you are, then don't lose sight of it. I've heard from many people that the returning person filled a lot of down time with exercise, so that was important. Be sure you take time to continue that and keep in shape.

65 Here's a thought: Be proactive, say what *you* want; *you* pick up the phone. Be honest. If you don't want to talk about prying questions that others have, say so.

66 Cheryl writes: "One suggestion I would have is not to do any real changes to the house while your deployed servicemember is gone. Unless this is something that you have both agreed upon, this is not a good idea. The main reason is that the deployed spouse has memories of what 'home' is and that's what they have held onto while away. If you change that, it may be too much for them, or it might even start an argument right away when they come home."

67 One woman said, "We had a Halloween party for everyone. It was fun and more leisurely." I like this because if you have a party on one of the "off" holidays then there isn't so much pressure on the family to make it perfect, like one might with Thanksgiving or Christmas. Halloween, Groundhog Day, and April Fool's Day come to mind. If you really want to have fun, and are at a loss for a holiday, check out the book *Chase's Calendar of Events* published by McGraw-Hill. You can find it at <u>Amazon.com</u> or your library. There are over 12,000 events/holidays listed by day and month so you can find anything you'd like to build a celebration around. There's a *National Bring your Teddy Bear to Work Day, National Chili Day* and even *National Rice Month!* Who knew that September has a *National Hat Day* or that May is *National Egg Month?* My mind goes nuts with the fun things you can make a party around; wearing funny hats, bringing your worst tie, or making all the party dishes out of eggs. So pick a day and go find something to celebrate.

68 Many times it was suggested that the family find a way to take a vacation together. The parameters are usually that it not happen immediately upon return, that the family discusses and agrees on the location, and that it doesn't "break the bank." After all, the main reason for this is to put less stress on the family, not more. One family found their way to Hawaii; another went camping in the mountains. It's totally up to you.

In regard to the vacation location, one family suggested that you go back to a familiar and favorite place that you went to and enjoyed before. That lends more comfort to the experience. Remember, too, that you truly don't have to go anywhere in order to be "on vacation." You really can just have time at home together without the pressure of schedules or obligations.

Note on vacations: When you are planning a vacation, be aware of busy locations and busy times of the year to visit. The idea of crowded, bustling places can be overwhelming to the person just returning from overseas. Part of combat stress can cause them to be uncomfortable and disoriented in overstimulated situations. I don't imagine that's the kind of vacation experience you're envisioning. Try taking a "lazy" vacation first.

Not all replies I received came in the form of an idea; some came as requests. I thought this one would apply to most of you.

69 "I would like a way to link up theme parks and/ or vacation spots to obtain discounts and/or multi-family trips for post-deployment togetherness time to put families together in a fun environment. This way they have time to work on their relationships with family members before facing the stress of home management."

I have good news for you. In the resource section in the back of this book, you'll find a section that lists some of the places that offer discounts and/or "freebies" to the military—at least at the time of printing. I hope you find something that sounds good to your family to begin your reunion.

The above thoughts and ideas will get you started on reconnecting with those around you. These reconnections will fit into their own time schedules. One of my favorite sayings is, "Take it to the Lord in prayer." When it seems like your family is at odds for longer than you think they should be, remember your faith and ask the "Higher Power" you believe in for help. Prayer and meditation can work wonders.

Dust off the "Little Black Book"— Back as a single soldier, airman, sailor or marine . . .

Much of this book is geared to the "married with children" demographic. I realize that many of those serving in the military are single. I'll take a few moments to share some thoughts that have been expressed to me concerning the return to single life following assignment or deployment. Most of the advice I heard was very similar to that for families, but a few differences did stand out.

The first is the support system that's in place for you upon return. Having parents, siblings and friends there for you is wonderful but can feel different from having a spouse and kids. That's okay, but you may find it harder to relate to your friends and relatives. More than likely, you may not have stayed connected with them with the frequency that you had hoped. So if you all feel a bit awkward at first, keep making the effort, and you should fall back in step with each other soon. Remember, they probably feel awkward, too.

Friends and extended family can't know as intimately as you what you have been through. Try to take some time to relate experiences in a more casual setting, and be patient with them. Help them to understand; be respectful of each other's feelings. Realize, too, that their circumstances may have changed. Some friends may have moved on—out of jobs or even the community. Their relationships with each other may have changed, too. Again, be prepared and patient. Life went on for them; now yours has to, as well. **Remember that you need to make an effort on your own behalf.** Help yourself to get back into the swing of things. Sometimes it's difficult to take the first step, but when others have moved on with their lives, that's what you need to do.

For the servicemember . . .

70 First, get your housing situated so that you begin to feel yourself reestablishing roots. Then you can begin to get other areas of your life back in order. Once you know where you'll be living, you can reevaluate your career goals based on your interests and financial needs. Maybe you'll be staying where you are, or maybe this is the time to make a change since you're a bit freer of relationship commitments. Looking ahead at where you can go with the support of friends and associates around you can be an exciting time of new beginnings.

71 You might be thinking of how soon you can get back "out there" with your friends, dating, etc. But remember to spend some time with your parents. As a parent, I know how much I worry about my sons, no matter what they're doing or where they are. Your parents worried about you, your welfare, and your safety for every minute you were gone. It's hard to live with that constant fear. If they live far away from you, then be sure to call frequently to let them know you're just fine. If they're within easy driving distance, then head over for Sunday dinner. If they don't live together, spend separate time with both.

What other advice does your military community have for you? Take a look:

72 Joyce says, "Go ahead and be good to yourself, but please be careful. Don't try to jam everything you want to do into the first couple of weeks that you're home." Trying to go at life with a sense of 'over kill' can backfire on you. Your aggressions are higher and more attuned now, and the littlest of things could set you off while with family and friends.

73 Partying with friends is great, but remember to watch your alcohol intake for the same reasons that are stated above.

74 I love this one! Darlene shared that the best way to feel like you're truly home is to pamper yourself because you can be sure no one did in Iraq! "As a woman, go get your hair done, get a manicure and pedicure, and of course you need a good massage." I'll add that this would be a great gift for a church group, friends, family, etc. to give to the returning servicewoman. Pay for her spa day.

75 The aggression issue reared it's ugly head again with advice from a chaplain. He said, "Please, try to curb your aggression by taking a minute to think out a situation before you react. Also, be sure to take it one day at a time."

While I was talking with a group of about 30 returning servicemembers about this issue, there were a lot of short answers shouted out about some things they have done that helped to get back into the swing of things when you're not surrounded by family. Here's what they said:

76 Get a pet!

77 Attend sporting events; better yet, join a sports team. It's great to get out and play a pick-up basketball game at a recreation center. One cool thing to do is to attend sporting events at your local high school, particularly if it's the one you attended. They'd love to see you, and you'll feel a real part of something. It's a wonderful place to watch a lot of love and support for others. Maybe consider volunteering as a team coach.

78 Learn something new. Update your computer skills, learn how to brew beer, or take a dance class—girls love it when a guy is a good dancer. There are lots of places to take free classes, and this is a great way to meet new people.

79 Volunteer in your community or with your FAC or FRG. You have lots of experience that others would love to learn from. How about a Big Brother or Big Sister program?

80 Join a health club. Keep yourself physically fit because the mind will stay alert, too. Pump out some of that aggression, and find yourself a "workout buddy" or someone you can run with in the mornings.

81 Finally, Glenn said to "Dust off that 'Little Black Book' and get back into the dating scene. It might not go great the first time, but feel free to practice . . . practice . . . practice!"

For your friends and loved ones . . .

82 Parents, please don't be too disappointed if your returning son or daughter isn't there at your house all the time, or even as much as you think they should be. I know you missed them more than you can say, but know that you are two of many people they want to spend time with. Have reasonable expectations and know that even though they are your children, they are also grown people who have gone off and done the work of a man or woman.

83 Dick told me that his single friend "Pete" returned from Iraq, so Dick set up a party with their friends and made sure Pete was there. It was great because it was an informal environment and gave Pete a chance to blend back in slowly. It also gave him a chance to talk to people one-on-one in a safe place.

84 It's been suggested that before your friend returns, you educate yourself on how he/she may have changed so it's not such a big shock. If you have a feeling of what you might expect, it will make your reunion go smoother.

85 Suzanne shared, "Talk to your friends and see if you can encourage them not to be 'intrusive' toward the returning servicemember. Sometimes a good friend should take a 'sit and wait' approach and be available when the servicemember needs or wants to talk. It just might take some time." Try not to bombard them with questions about what happened "over there."

"I'm sure we can make this work."— Dealing with changed roles at home . . .

The good news is . . . your spouse is coming home! The bad news is . . . your spouse is coming home! You're starting to realize that getting back on track might not be as easy as it sounds. Things sure have changed around here while they were gone—some for the better and some not so much. This topic of changed roles has been a big one when I lead small group discussions. I see so much new-found independence at home and a concern for how the returning people see themselves fitting back in. Feelings of anxiety and nervousness are normal for everyone because of those changes. You might wonder, *Will they still need me and love me? . . . be proud of me?* And all the while the spouse at home is enjoying some of the new responsibility and strength they've found in themselves.

Often this new self-esteem actually becomes part of who they are, and they don't want to give it up right away, if at all. It sounds like some work has to be done to find that middle ground where each of your needs can be met. What I found interesting was that opinions on this topic varied from, "You have to go back to the old ways," to "Just accept the new way, and find a way to blend in!" So who's to say who's right and who's wrong? Just take a look at what others are offering, apply your own personal situation to it, and I'll bet you'll find some pearls of wisdom.

86 Before they even come home, take turns discussing role changes that have occurred. Talk about which ones you might want to consider going back to and which to change. If the discussion is initially started before you're back together, it will give it time to "sink in." One woman told me that she and her husband talked about role changes way back before he ever even left for Iraq. Of course, some things might have changed or adjusted as the time went on, but her husband felt that it "lightened his worry load" knowing what was going on at home.

87 "Once home," Mary said, "my husband liked it when I still remained somewhat of a buffer between him and the outside world for a while. He said that it was really great that I answered the phone, and he only had to deal with conversations he chose."

88 "Don't be disappointed if your returning spouse feels a little 'hurt' that you got along so well without him/her as far as handling the household. Let him/her know that yes, it went well, but it was a lot of work, and you're looking forward to sharing some of the responsibilities again."

89 "One thing that helped my husband was to show my appreciation for the little things he does around the house. When he was gone I became fairly self-sufficient, and it was hard to let go of the reins and let him have a part in managing the household again. It was a process; I didn't want him to feel overwhelmed, but still I wanted him to know that he was missed and appreciated." This is kind of like finding our kids doing something right and letting them know about it. Why is it that we are so quick to pick up on what someone is doing wrong and telling them rather than "catching" them doing something right.

90 Speaking of catching someone doing something right, if your spouse "stepped up" while you were gone and effectively took charge, recognize it for the gift it was intended to be—that his/her "stepping up" let you do your job!

91 MSG Barbara shares, "Don't try to catch up on Day One. The spouses who did not deploy are very independent and now set in their ways. The military members who deployed must understand that their spouses are used to doing things their own way now. Both must learn to get back to doing things together as a team."

Everyone expects roles to change, but be aware that each of your own personal interests and opinions may have changed or at least been altered, too. That could be a surprise when conversations change. Here are some areas that most often are affected:

- Political views (but less than most)

- Religious beliefs (especially if there was an injury or traumatic experience involved either overseas or at home)

- Ideas about career

- Ideas about money

- Preferences in books, movies, music, clothes and image (what's up with that tattoo?!)

92 One man wrote, "I took a step back to observe how things were being done rather than jump in and take control. The first time I had returned from deployment, I tried to jump right into my previous role, but realized a little late that things were being done better! That's why I smartened up the second time."

93 Talk, talk, talk . . . about changes. Be open to renegotiating your expectations.

94 "Don't expect your deployed loved one to start helping around the house and with the kids right away. Give him/her a 'vacation' at home for a week or two. Then they'll start blending back in more on their own. It's nice when the decision to help comes from them in their own time."

95 "When I was deployed, I found it hard to adjust to not being able to see my family every day. I would write a letter to them each day telling them what I was experiencing. I wouldn't send the letter until I had a few days of them written. This helped my family feel closer to me. Upon returning home, I did not try to make drastic changes; I eased back into the role of being a parent and spouse. For a while my spouse continued to make some of the major decisions. I eventually took over these roles after a couple of months back. My spouse continued to be the disciplinarian of my child, and I eased back into that role, too, after getting used to being an at-home parent again."

96 I thought this was a great idea. It was offered in a small group session I was facilitating at a readiness conference this past summer. When I posed the question of how to adjust to your new normal, one woman spoke up and said it was a good idea to "wear the other person's shoes." Well of course I thought she meant figuratively, but no, she meant that they literally wore each others shoes! They switched shoes, and while they were wearing the shoes they talked about what it must have been like to be the person in those shoes during the deployment. She said that in a fun way it helped each of them see what the other must have felt like while living their life.

97 One family did a complete turnaround. Similar to "wearing each other's shoes," they reassigned roles so each had the chance to actually experience what went on at home and how things were handled. They did this only after a couple of weeks. These new roles were different from what they were doing before the deployment. It let Dad see what it was like to drive the kids to school, games, music lessons, and to decide what's for dinner. It let Mom deal with all of the maintenance, finances, and the cable company (which is pretty much what she did while he was gone anyway!) But it was a good eye opener.

The following is an interesting example of a family taking what was learned "in theatre" and applying it to an "at home" situation.

98 "The military member conducts what they call a 'left seat, right seat' ride with their counterpart as they prepare to depart the theatre of operations and redeploy home. This allows a specific amount of time for the outgoing person to show the incoming person what is expected of them in this particular job. Then the roles are reversed, and while the outgoing person is still in theatre, the incoming person starts to conduct business as if he/she was now in charge. This allows time for questions to be asked while the outgoing person is still available in theatre.

We adopted a similar scenario at home. Instead of the minute he walked through the door me giving back all the responsibilities to my husband that he had prior to the deployment, we established a time line where I would continue to take care of things (i.e.; the finances, household chores, auto maintenance, etc.) while he watched. Then when he felt comfortable in his daily routine, he would slowly take back over the things he did before the deployment. This way I was still available to assist if problems arose. What we discovered is that I retained some of the tasks that he used to do, and he decided to take back others. By being patient and openly communicating how we feel about certain things, we have been able to come up with a system that works in our home that makes things run very smoothly. There are just certain things that I would rather he do, and certain things he would rather I do."

99 Here's another viewpoint: "If it ain't broke, don't fix it! If a system has been working well while you're gone, you don't have to change it back to the way it was before."

That's a good reminder, Joel. I think that works best when it's the result of observing what's been happening in your absence.

To the servicemember: A caveat to this advice is for you to be observant and willing to take over if the at-home person is ready to let the task go. Remember, he/she might be hanging on by a thread.

So what shines through all these examples? Patience, communication and observation. Your household isn't a dictatorship, it's a democracy—or at least close to it! The more people feel their input is being considered, the easier it is to find common ground. Remember, you're normal, and you're going to do just fine as you fit your roles together like a jigsaw puzzle. In the end, you'll like the picture it makes.

"I didn't mean it that way!"—
It's a communication thing . . .

If there's one thing that comes through loud and clear in ideas throughout the entire book, it's the idea that many problems can be solved through open communication. I hear it all the time, and it makes perfect sense.

If you're a person who has ever watched "soap operas" (or as my grandmother used to refer to them, her "stories") or prime time dramas, admit it right now. Go ahead, you know who you are! Most of us at one time or another have found ourselves wrapped up in the television lives of others. I used to watch "All My Children." Many years ago when I was in college, our dormitory lounge was filled with girls at 3:00 p.m. for that day's episode of "General Hospital." See? You're in good company. As you're watching a conflict unfold, have you ever said to the TV, "Why don't you guys just talk about it? He's mad because he doesn't know how you really feel!" or something of that nature. I know I have. It seems so obvious to us sitting on the outside that people just have to talk it out; then they can get on with their lives. But then of course, if they did that, there wouldn't be any storyline.

The idea is the same in real life, which is why I like this chapter so much. People just need to talk. Yes, I know, easier said than done. At least that's the way it seems sometimes.

Personally, I think it would help if I could "just know" what kind of a mood the other person is in at any given moment so I would know if this would be a good time to talk. Sometimes I bring something up at a time when I think we should talk, but it becomes evident that Larry doesn't feel the same way! So then I go away mad because he snapped at me. I'm pretty sure this scenario goes on other homes, too, which is why I share my own experience:

On Halloween day, we went to the costume party in my granddaughter's first grade classroom. We stood back along the wall and watched all the commotion and excitement of a bunch of kids getting pumped up on sugar and treats! I turned around behind me and saw a fabric poster on the wall with pockets all over the front of it—one for each student. Inside each pocket were five brightly colored laminated slips of paper with a couple of words printed on each one as follows:

Green—Excellent Day ☺

Yellow—Good Day

Purple—At Risk

White—Warning!

Red—Code RED

I asked about these messages and the teacher smiled. She said that at any time during the day the children could pull a slip out of the pocket that reflected what kind of a day they were having and put it on the table in front of them. This helped her get a glimpse into any possible reasons for behavior challenges or maybe just overly talkative episodes. She was able to be more observant to times when her help or care might be needed. How great it would be for us all if we were able to "see into" our loved ones and get a feel for how to communicate best at that moment, or to just leave them alone for a while.

I'd love to be able to pin one of those mood papers on my clothing on some mornings! Jenn says that she has a tee shirt that says "Grumpy!" on it, and she wears it on days that she's just not feeling all that "approach-able." I think that's a great idea! How can you talk to someone who "clams up" or shuts you down? How long do you let someone just "stew" over something before you insist that they talk to you?

These are great questions and some of the ideas and exercises offered in the next few pages should help with that. Lots of people have been through it, and maybe what worked to get people talking can work for you, too.

100 It's harder to fix something that was broken to begin with. That means that you have to maintain a healthy level of communication throughout the deployment by writing letters or emails or calling when possible. Don't let time get in the way of com-munication.

101 "I've learned that compromise can be a true art form! Deployments give both of you separate tasks and missions you need to complete successfully. Now that you're home, it's time to learn about sharing again."

102 Amanda wrote, "When my husband came home from his first deployment I had decorated the outside of the house with huge banners, lights, everything. But what I wasn't prepared for was just how different my husband was when he came home. He was still the same man I fell in love with, but his personality was different at first. He didn't like to talk about being over there, but we worked through that by talking every night about how each other was feeling no matter if it was difficult or not. This helped us reconnect and stay bonded because although the intimacy was there immediately, which was great, the communication and learning to talk again was the most important part. You change a lot in a year. You can reconnect if you just work at it. He is gone for his second tour now, which will be a whole new experience when he comes home because we now have two young sons."

When we have a good relationship with someone, we usually believe that we know that person "inside and out." You know those couples who can finish each other's sentences. Guess what, each of us brought who we were to the relationship, too. Most people call that "baggage," but it's still a part of who we are. Sometimes it's difficult to see around that baggage to get to the real reasons why people feel the way they do about something. Many of us have looked at our partner in puzzlement and asked, "How can you possibly feel that way?" Trying to understand that is often where good communication begins. Here's my advice:

103 Don't be too critical of why people feel the way they do about something. Maybe they really don't know why they feel a certain way, or it's buried somewhere yet is a foundation piece for who they are now. If this sounds a bit complicated, let me share a story of mine that might explain it better.

"Man, I hate white!" I said in frustration.

My husband, Larry, and I had just bought a new house. I'm standing in the middle of the living room—stark, barren and so "white." In fact, every room was "new house" white.

"What do you mean you don't like white?" Larry shot back at me, actually astounded by my statement. "How can you not like white?" I had to think about that one. I was arguing with a man who wanted every room to stay white because to him, it has a "nice clean" look. He didn't even want me to put pictures on the walls! I couldn't imagine this ending well at all.

Why *don't* I like white in my surroundings? I never have; it makes me uncomfortable. There has to be a reason. Then it begins to appear like it's emerging from a haze of neglect and forgetfulness. Psychologists say that we usually form our earliest memories around the time we start school. It gives us something to "attach" them to. For me it's different. I remember being three.

I'm small. I'm dressed up like I'm going to church, yet I'm not. I have on a wool coat that comes to my knees and a matching hat. It's raining out and I'm holding onto my mom's hand while we walk through a parking lot toward a door up ahead. I try to avoid the puddles because I have on "good shoes." I'm walking kind of fast because it takes about three of my steps to keep up with a single one of Mom's. We finally reach the door and walk through it into a hallway. I remember that there was a lot of activity going on and no one was really paying any attention to me. Mom just kept holding my hand. It's not easy figuring out what's happening when you can only see "knees"—and white. I noticed that the floor of this hallway was white, marred only occasionally by scuff marks. The walls were white, too, and white shiny tile as far up as I could see. I could also see white skirts. And there was crying and tense talking. (You know how you can just feel tenseness?) That's all I remember about that moment—crying and white.

Many years later I learned that my dad had gone into the hospital for open heart surgery and for about four minutes he had "died." It was that news that the nurses were giving my mother that day when I was three in the waiting area of the hospital. I'm glad to say that he made it through that surgery and went on to live a great life. So much later it became obvious to me why I don't like the color white. Too many bad memories are attached to it and they came rushing back that afternoon in the living room of my new house.

Why do I think it's important for you to share in my story? Because it shows how each one of us has things that are buried that can shoot back to the surface and account for how we feel or how we react to something. I can only imagine what traumatic events are experienced by our servicemembers if they are in a combat zone, and any one of those can trigger things that are uncomfortable to talk about. You, as a loved one, need to be patient and caring as things unfold. Try to talk about the reasons beneath the issue that can lead to certain behaviors. Let them know that you're trying to understand and that you care.

In my living room that day, Larry gave me the chance to talk about why I hate white. He didn't think it was silly or laugh at me. He understood, although he still thought it strange. We compromised and painted the interior walls a soft beige color. It took the "sting" out of white and still has a nice clean look. I have to tell you that we agreed on some pictures for the walls, too!

104 Heather wrote to me about three things that she believes summarize some of the general principles behind effectively communicating with each other:

TAKE TIME. Take time for you as an individual. Give your soldier time to themselves, and give them space with each child. Then take time as a couple to begin the rebuilding of your relationship.

PATIENCE. Have patience with each other. The separation has caused changes in each member of the family, and patience is needed by everyone (especially the adults) with everyone they come in contact with.

UNDERSTANDING. Understand that the other person may not understand what has changed. Take time to discuss even the little things. This is something that definitely needs to be in play when meeting with outside family members because they want to "know" everything that went on while the soldier was away. (This can be true especially for the soldiers who may not be ready to discuss with anyone the details of what they have been through.)

Since my books are filled with ideas that come from others who are going through what you are, here are some things I heard that people do during and after deployment to try to keep communication problems small. It's sort of like making a preemptive strike.

105 "Whenever my husband deploys, I stuff 'love notes' in every nook and cranny, pocket, boot, etc. I also do that when he is here so he gets the message that I love him even when he's home." Now that's a message that can't be over stated!

106 Keeping close is a two way street, as Jennifer tells us, "While deployed, my husband attended marriage enrichment courses in Iraq. This helped him stay connected to me. Then when he returned, we met with a PREP (Prevention Relationship Enrichment Program) advisor. We try to meet with the counselor every four to six weeks. It has really helped us to reconnect and grow as a team."

Author's note: We'll be talking more about PREP and Strong Bonds in the section on Intimacy and Image.

107 I always like it when Julie sends me something. I've used a lot of her ideas in my newsletter. "Have just plain family time, no plans or expectations. Take walks, go to the park, get ice cream, play silly board games." As far as talking when you're together, she suggests, "Don't rehash the deployment over and over, and the time your loved one spent in country. Stay focused on the events that occurred— after all, what they did there matters, and what their comrades are continuing to do still matters. We discuss the current events and have sent a couple of care packages to 'adopt a soldier' because even though he is home now, it is not over for so many!"

108 Jenn says, "If your husband (or any service-member) is like mine, he usually won't just talk about things all on his own. He needs to have a door opened. So every once in a while when he seems withdrawn or stressed, I'll say something that will give him an outlet to begin talking. Then I let him know that he has my full attention, like sitting down next to him and just waiting. Most of the time this is the 'invitation' he needs to let some things out. I try to make him feel safe."

109 This idea from Tonya follows along with the ideas that talk about keeping deployment journals, but this adds a different twist to it and is done for a different reason. "My husband is currently deployed to Iraq. We have four sons ages eight to twelve. To help our soldier ease back into the 'family life,' we have made books. Each child has his own and so do I. They are filled with pictures from birthdays, holidays, and a lot of 'just everyday' shots. We write stories to go along with the pictures and also write about our feelings at the time. We all, including my husband, keep journals to be shared with each other. It helps us see where each other is emotionally and mentally. It has really helped all of us stay connected in the same way as before the deployment. Our soldier doesn't come home until mid-year, and so far it has been a great idea. I'm able to look at the books and journal so I can catch and try to resolve any issues that may come up. That way, they are not problems when he comes home. I hope this idea will help someone the way it has helped our family."

110 Amanda writes, "When answering questions from other people, you just need to stop and think before you speak because you don't want to say anything that is confidential, and sometimes whatever emotion you are feeling at that moment can cause you to say things you wouldn't normally say. Just pause and collect your thoughts first. If you don't want to really answer the questions (and you don't have to) you can just say, 'He's okay,' or 'We are just your normal deployment family.'"

Now let's move on to some things to do once you're in the conversation to keep it sane. I've taught classes on effective communication so I might be able to shed some light along with what others have said. I've discovered that we really do know what to do and how to act, it's just difficult when our egos or emotions are involved. I remember someone telling me once that we are so much nicer to our friends and casual acquaintances than we are to the people we love the most. They were right. We tend to think about what we're going to say and "how it will sound" to our friends, but to our spouse, parents, kids, etc., we just let them have it with whatever's on our minds.

I think of this every time I hear a teenager yell, "I hate you!" to a parent. But I guess that's just human nature. I'll bet things would be a lot better if we talked to our spouse like we would to a friend. Which brings me to one of the best pieces of advice I have heard over the past few years. It comes from a participant in a conference breakout session called, *The **good** news is your spouse is home . . . the **bad** news is your spouse is home.* Here it is:

111 "My husband and I have been best friends since high school. Sometimes our discussions can get pretty heated because there can be so much emotion involved. When we get to the point where it appears that we just can't go any further because no one is listening anymore, I step back and say, 'I just can't talk to you as my spouse anymore, so I want to talk to you as my best friend.' Then we sit down as friends, not spouses. I have to tell you, it works almost every time."

112 Robert has three thoughts on communication to share. "First, the eyes have it. To me that means that each of you has to have two eyes in the conversation. That ensures that you are totally focused and listening as well as talking. You're paying attention. Next, if your discussion is getting way too emotional, break away and write down your issue(s). Then give it to the other person and leave her/him alone to think about it. Sometimes when you're reading what another person is feeling, you can see their side more objectively. After that you can usually talk about it easier. You also might try having a discussion in a public place like a coffee shop or something. Being in view of others can help keep things from escalating into a shouting match."

113 A couple of rules or guidelines for good conversations came out at one of the breakouts and they're good to tuck away:

- Practice silent listening. This means to listen to what the other person is saying, wait for them to completely finish their thought (do not finish their statements for them), then repeat back what you heard them say. This is called word check. You do this to verify the facts (not emotions) and be sure that you have a clear understanding of what they are saying. It's kind of hard to do this a lot, so practice it for a while and when you think it's getting "silly," stop for a while, although finding something silly can be a good thing!

- Another side of listening is to be sure there are no distractions like the TV or computer while you're talking. Above all, this shows respect for the other person.

- You can use "I feel . . ." statements to occasionally help get your feelings out. How often we just feel misunderstood or taken for granted. Being able to tell your loved one how you feel (frustrated, angry, sad) can start the conversation.

- Always be honest and open with the other person. Good conversations come from a point of trust. Be sincere.

Two closing thoughts about communication:

114 Here's a great way for the returning service-person to let their loved one at home know how much their work and sacrifice was appreciated during the deployment. After all, she's probably thinking, *I didn't sign up for this!* When nothing is distracting you, maybe over a coffee or cocktail, you might mention, "Tell me what it was like while I was gone." Then shut up and listen! You can ask this of any family member because they all had different experiences. That lets you get a closer look at how your family held together.

As in most marriages, Larry and I had a period of time when we were drifting apart and always seemed to be fighting about everything! We decided to talk to a marriage counselor, which turned out to be a good thing. Sometimes the hardest part is to admit that you need some help. I remember sitting there talking about how frustrating it was to be fighting all the time, and the counselor actually said that he was relieved about that;

it was a good thing! He said, "Believe it or not, if you're arguing, you probably still care enough to work on making things better. It's a bad sign if a couple comes in who have gone past arguing and now just don't care. That's more difficult to fix." I imagine that makes a lot of you feel better about where you are.

"How the heck did my butt get so big?"— Image, intimacy, sex and other challenges of being a couple

This is it. This is the time you've been waiting for—getting back into the swing of things. Low and behold, it might not be as easy as you thought. But it can get back on the right track if you're ready to give it a little time. One thing to remember is that sex and intimacy aren't really the same thing. Intimacy was the closeness that you maintained while you were apart. In my deployment book, *I'm Already Home . . . Again*, I called it "making love across the miles." It was intimacy that you expressed through love notes, special photos, or special intimations of what to expect after deployment. Intimacy is what brought the smile to your face. Sex is that wonderful connection that you have now that you're both in the same place! It's picking up where you left off, or at least trying to. Some of that depends on how you each feel about yourself personally. Let's talk about that.

First, I want you to like yourself! The story I shared in the beginning of the book about the woman who declared, upon hearing that her husband was coming home, "How the heck did my butt get so big?" is how so many feel. It doesn't matter if you're a man or woman, you never think that you look as good as you should for yourself or your partner. It's hard to feel sexy when you're convinced that you don't look that way. How come we're never tall enough, thin enough (there's just more of you to love), or pretty enough in our own eyes? Must be human nature.

So, what are you going to do about it? Crash diets aren't the answer. So my advice is: do what you can in the time you have (a few extra pushups, toss the ice cream, or maybe an updated haircut), and then appreciate yourself for who you are and know that your loved one just wants to love **you**. Yes, it's true! We're so hard on ourselves and think that we have to look perfect all the time. Guess what, you've both changed physically, and like they say, love is blind—and that's the way it's supposed to be. So lighten up, enjoy the way you look now, and know that you are the gift you're giving back to each other after being apart for so long.

No matter what you do to light that fire again, remember to have realistic expectations. There's a lot of pressure on both of you to rekindle the flames in the same way that you did a year earlier. Only this time you're really anxious! Remember:

115 It just might not be as earth shattering as you were expecting right at the beginning. You're both probably a bit nervous and that stress can bring about some difficulties with "performance." After you've determined that there aren't any physical changes or medical reasons/injuries, please just go with the flow and take pressure off of each other. If it's a bit awkward now, trust me, it will get better with practice. Give it time and don't jump to unfounded conclusions like it must be that he doesn't love me anymore.

Also, if you remember from your early relationship years, men and women approach sex differently (duh). Because sex is more than a physical act for most women, you men might consider creating a romantic environment, and make sure the emotional part of sex is being taken care of. I remember once my husband telling me that in his view men have sex to build to the romance and emotion, and women have to have the emotion to get to the sex. I know that sounds simplistic, and it doesn't apply to everyone, but there seem to be a lot of opinions about it.

116 Based on our differences as men and women, might I suggest that you head into this with the notion of building the intimacy again first, which should lead back to the sex life you enjoyed.

◆

**A book that was recommended is
*Sex Begins in the Kitchen:
Because Love is an All-Day Affair*
by Dr. Kevin Leman.
His message has a Christian foundation,
but according to a review, it isn't churchy.
Go to *Amazon.com* and check it out for yourself
to see if it's right for you.**

◆

**How about starting with 1001 ideas!
Get a copy of *1001 Ways to be Romantic*
by Gregory Godek.
You'll find it at most bookstores or on *Amazon.com*.
From simple ideas like writing "I love you"
on the bathroom mirror with a piece of soap,
to filling your lover's car with balloons,
to more steamy ideas when you're ready—it will
help turn your marriage back into a love affair!**

◆

117 Speaking of a love affair, try dating again. That's when feelings were new, much as they are now after a long separation. Remember back to what attracted you to each other in the first place. What little things did you do for each other that made you so endearing? Those are the original feelings that became your wonderful relationship. Jean said that she and her husband established a date night before he came home. They picked a date and they talked about where they would go and what to do. It was fun for them to plan it together and look forward to it during that time.

To help you find fun things to do anytime together, sit and make some lists.

- List 1: Things that are free or very inexpensive

- List 2: Things that are quick and you can do "on a whim"

- List 3: Those things or places that take more time and effort, or are more expensive so you have to plan and save

Keep these lists in an accessible location so you can whip them out anytime you want something to do.

This idea of dating works great for so many families. Here's what Irma says about dating and what they told the kids:

118 "When my husband came back we made an effort to have dates with each other. We explained to our kids that Mommy and Daddy needed alone time to learn about ourselves again without them. Our seven-year-old had a hard time dealing with the concept, and I told her that in a few years she would be in high school and then graduate from school. We told her that when she and her brother left home to start their lives, Mommy and Daddy would only have each other. It was important for Mommy and Daddy to have dates with each other to stay in love so that we will stay with each other long after they leave home. My kids understand now, and my husband and I have tried to go on at least two dates a month, since his return. It has made a world of difference, and I look forward to getting ready to go out with my husband."

Here's another way to keep the romance strong during deployment and beyond:

119 "I sent a 'message in a bottle' to my hubby in Iraq. I wrote a love letter on textured card stock using a calligraphy pen. I made it look old by distressing it (scrapbooking technique) and perfumed it. I put the letter in a clear plastic bottle, sealed it and mailed it to Iraq. It took about a month to get there but it did arrive. He thought it was super cool and was very impressed. It was a lot of fun."

Another woman did something like this, too, and wrote to tell me that her husband wrote her a love letter back, placed it in the same bottle and brought it home to her. He floated it in her bathtub!

120 After about two or three months following the return home, the two of you need to get away for a weekend to a nice resort or location that has each of your favorite activities (like golf, shopping, touring, etc.). It's vital to reconnect on your own, but also important that you don't jump right into this immediately. If you allow two to three months, you'll find that you're more comfortable with each other and might feel less guilt about leaving the kids again right away. Can't afford a "getaway weekend?" I know that many Chaplain services are sponsoring these weekends as they can. Ask of other programs available, too, like dinner cruises. I know they're out there. It's a gift to your kids to love each other.

What are others doing that could spark your own creativity?

121 Cynthia brings up another way to use that time away together. "I know my hubby and I had a few issues with intimacy and communication when I came home from Afghanistan. The home front seemed to be his 'area.' We had no neutral ground. So we came up with an idea to spend some weekends away from home without the children, although we did go on vacation as a family. We planned a three- or four-day weekend for just the two of us. We took out a map, rolled a die (each number represented a direction) and drove. Sometimes the drive was only an hour or so; sometimes it was quite a few hours. Then whatever our fancy was, we would stop in one place for the rest of the weekend. The drive helped us talk and reestablish our communication, while the weekend away helped us discover each other once again. We still do it at least once every other month. We have worked out quite a few problems this way."

122 Amanda says, "Husbands and wives need time to themselves. That is why they need to get someone to watch their kids for at least one to three days so they can get to know each other again before they get thrown back into full family life. I believe the bond between Mommy and Daddy helps with taking care of the kids and other important parts in any family. You need time to get back to knowing your husband or your wife without any outside interferences. I call this a little honeymoon phase, which is what many other wives and I believe is somewhat critical."

I really like what Amanda said because I agree strongly that the special, unique bond you have as husband and wife is, and should be, different from the bond with your children. In the deployment speaking session I do at state conferences, I talk about intimacy transcending miles. I tell parents that I know how much you want to be with your kids when you first return, but you must understand that no matter how important your family is, that family began with **the two of you!** There's nothing wrong with letting your kids see the strength and bond you have as a couple. Children need to feel "safe" emotionally in their home and to know that home is a stable place of love.

123 Jodi reminds us, "Many spouses wait until their kids go to bed for their time alone. A few hours are not enough time, and the returning spouse is often extremely tired. This can lead the other spouse to feel neglected and add to the 'there is a stranger in my bed' feeling. So give yourself the freedom to be together alone! I wish I would have done that for every deployment return!"

Finally, while facilitating a group session in Phoenix, we ended up with a whole list of "one line" ideas that people said worked for them to "set the mood" and get things going. I decided to just list them here. I think you'll get a kick out of them and realize that you've probably done these too, which makes you normal!

- Think creatively.

- Remember the time factor; don't rush, if possible.

- Watch for competition for your attention, such as the kids, the TV, and other environmental distractions.

- For romance, try an adult "boutique shop."

- Schedule your time alone.

- Liquor—in moderation and only for those who can handle it.

- Tell each other how you feel.

- Talk about the first time you met.

- Take a walk together.

- Get a hotel room with a deep tub!

- Be respectful of one another.

- Give each other a massage.

- Bubbles—a bath and champagne.

- Show constant, subtle, verbal and non-verbal signs of affection.

And my favorite (in his exact words)

- "Dim the lights, light a candle, and go at it like rabbits!"

Not sure I can do better than that; seems like a good place to move ahead.

We talk a lot about communication in the book because so much of what happens between people comes down to this. Sometimes, no matter how hard you try, you feel like you just aren't getting through to your spouse. I'm sure you've never had to have a conversation with a pigheaded individual you just happen to love. Marion told me that once she got so exasperated with her husband that she just blurted out, "What part of 'I Love You' don't you get?!" She said that to her surprise, it lightened things up a bit and the conversation went on in a better direction because the love was secure in his mind.

P.S. Keep in mind that if you try all you can and things are going nowhere, or there are more serious issues involved like infidelity, lost love feelings, or serious changes in your circumstances, please run to your nearest avenue for counseling or other kinds of help. There are many resources in the back of this book for places to start, and you can always find assistance and guidance at your Chaplain's office and at MilitaryOneSource.com. Please don't let it simmer because it's bound to eventually boil over.

Many of you know that I speak my mind. I'm going to talk about God. So if this bothers or offends you, skip ahead and rejoin us after the next three paragraphs. But I hope you'll hang in there instead, especially if your marriage is having some problems.

My husband and I recently saw the film *Fireproof*. We have a decent marriage, and it still held some wonderful secrets to putting each other first—after our relationship with God—that we had forgotten about. It was wonderful to see a film that showcased real heros, in real marriages, with real issues. It was wonderful to see a film that had the guts to talk openly about your relationship with God. It was wonderful to see a film that actually gave you a path to help make your marriage better and recognized that you have to take responsibility for it.

Many of us think that we can do everything ourselves without needing any help. In fact, it's feared that looking for professional help may carry a stigma to it that will follow you. As a result, those who truly should get outside help tend not to. Big mistake! I'm seeing that the military is getting better in this area as they make more private counseling and services available.

That's what I like about falling back on a relationship with God. Prayer can happen anytime, anywhere, and it carries no stigma because it's between you and God— oh, and maybe a family member or two. *Fireproof* also shows that there is no quick fix. You have to be willing to save and hold dear to what you have. My advice here is to go rent *Fireproof* and do the "Love Dare" if you want as a couple. At the time of printing, you can go to www.fireproofmymarriage.com and find information about the film and materials about the "Love Dare."

124 Attend a PREP (Prevention and Relationship Enrichment Program) or Strong Bonds marriage enrichment weekend. One of the best parts is that they are usually held at very nice resorts, and it's a perfect opportunity for the two of you to get away together with other couples to enjoy the time and experience ideas for strengthening your relationship. This is not therapy, so guys, you can feel comfortable attending.

Another big thing to remember, especially when you're trying to "sell" it to the man in your life is that this is not a Christian-based program. It's secular, so it works within all faiths and belief systems. This is important to point out because most of the programs are organized and run by chaplains. About a year ago I did some research on PREP in my usual way; I interviewed many couples who had attended and asked them what they thought. I received many responses and put them in a feedback report. I'm going to list some of the biggest "pluses" that couples felt about the weekend to start you thinking about what to expect. If you'd like the entire report (it's a Microsoft Word document), log in at www.ImAlreadyHome.com and you'll find a link to that document. In no particular order, here are some responses to the question:

How did the PREP marriage enrichment help your relationship most?

- I like that it makes the other person feel important.

- Speaker/listener techniques and how to improve both (multiple responses)

- How to make forgiveness easier, and reconciliation afterwards easier, too

- Better communication skills (#1 positive response)

- We learned to value our time together.

- We will actually use the skills and techniques we were taught because they were real and down to earth.

- It helped us to address personal issues.

- Conflict resolution/management

- Staying sensual in your everyday life

- It forced us to "play" and spend uninterrupted time with each other. This was the first time that our time together didn't involve our kids, my school, volunteering, his job, and other people's needs. We actually were required to have fun; thus we were forced to spend time actually talking. That was by far the most beneficial aspect of the weekend.

- The most frequent comment I hear from spouses is how much their husband benefited from the info on communication, specifically how men and women differ in their communication styles. I've had military wives tell me that they believe attending a seminar saved their marriage. When a husband turns to his wife and says, "I had no idea that when I said ____, you might have heard ____. I'm so sorry." The marriage enrichment seminars are a great help during this time of constant deployments when communication is strained and often in the form of e-mails or short telephone conversations. The better the family communicates, the better their chances to preserve the marriage.

- It was a great tool in helping us relearn how to communicate with each other. I think that if couples go into the seminar to make it a learning experience, it will be; if they are going just to get a weekend away, although they may not get a lot from the seminar, it will have given them time to themselves.

- The one thing that I can say is that if you go into it thinking that it is going to solve your problems for you, you are going in for the wrong reason. Like anything that's worth having, your marriage is work, for both partners.

- I believe that it would be very beneficial to returning soldiers. My wife and I had a hard time for about the first month and half of my return, but everything is about to get settled down. This is something that I feel should be pushed harder.

- We've rediscovered "dating" each other and make it a point to go out on a "date" at least once a week. We have also learned about each other's love language so that each of us knows what really makes the other feel loved and appreciated.

- We discovered how to recognize the different emotions that may happen while the soldier is deployed and how to keep him/her connected to the home front, especially after returning.

- The best part for me was learning how to listen so I could really understand what my husband, as well as our children, were saying. Assumptions are a big problem and definitely inhibit listening to someone you love. Thinking you know what your spouse is going to say and assuming you know how they feel, well, you are usually wrong. The listening tools were the best thing I have ever learned to use, and I try to get my adult children to use them also.

- The nicest part was that we weren't under a microscope. We were not judged, pushed into anything, forced to reveal things we didn't want to publicly, etc.

- They kept a very difficult subject light and easy going. Everyone shared and joked and that helped keep things upbeat and manageable.

- Learning how to communicate more openly was a big thing that we both picked up on from the seminar. I, especially, am one to immediately get defensive instead of remaining calm and talking things through. We each had changed a lot during the deployment and that was a big adjustment in working out the details—to once again become a married couple and learn how to work together as a couple.

- It was a great experience in that it allowed us "couple time." It brought into focus the right way to listen to your partner, and we still use the "I've got the floor" method when we really need to get our spouse to listen to what we have to say. Sometimes when they have been gone so long, it seems like we have to talk like we did on the rare phone calls—as fast as you can so you can get everything in.

- I think that it was very good for my husband to see that other couples have the same problems and some have even bigger problems than ours. Two of his buddies also attended the program with their wives and since being back from Iraq, he enjoys any time he can spend with any of the guys who were over there with him.

- We didn't realize that we were not listening to each other. Let me clarify that each of us knew that the other was not listening, but neither of us realized that we were not listening to the other. Yes, we do still disagree and have arguments, but we now have a better time understanding the other person's point of view and resolving our conflicts.

- The best part of the program was that it was pre-sented by local National Guard clergymen who understood our lives outside of just being married.

- The night before the program started we did a round table exercise that allowed us each to meet and greet a handful of the other participants. That really helped to go into the session not feeling like we were the only ones that could use some new skills.

- Biggest part of the program that has made a difference for us is that family is stressed here back at home and that it's also stressed in Iraq. My hubby said that they get talks about what we are going through and how there is a war going on back home.

At the time this survey was taken, the program was in its early stages. I'm finding now that it's becoming much more available in all branches of the service. Another response I heard a lot was that you should attend this as soon as possible after your return. Don't wait a couple of months or more because you don't want to give problems a chance to settle in. If you're going to learn great techniques to make your marriage better, then why not begin to use them right away?

Strong Bonds and the exercises provided will set the foundation for getting you to continue communicating with each other about the issues that really matter. It prepares you for the things that try to chip away at that foundation. It's never been a surprise that sex and money are the two biggest things that can cause relationships to crumble.

"I can't believe how much you've changed!"— Children and reunion . . .

How exciting this time can be for you all. As a parent, I understand that there is pretty much nothing harder than being apart from your children for so long. Right now you can be glad that you took the time to find ways to stay connected with each other over these past months. This is when it pays off. Your children and you have gone through two big areas of change: being separated and now coming back together. Each takes its own getting used to.

So much of the ease or disruption of returning home can depend on the relationship you had before you left and the age of the children. Little ones are so resilient and find they can adapt to new situations and surroundings. This is great while you're gone, but when you come back it takes them longer to adjust. That can be disappointing if they are a bit distant at first. Please give it time. Trust me, it won't take as long as you think. Keep in mind that not all children will follow patterns, and you may only observe sporadic behavior changes. The following reference list is provided by a State Youth Coordinator to help better understand this transition:

Birth to 1 Year
- Cries, fusses, pulls away from you
- Clings to other parent/caregiver
- Change in sleep and/or eating habits
- Does not recognize you—"out of sight, out of mind"

How to Respond:
- Let your baby set the pace.
- Hold and hug your baby as much as he/she is comfortable with.
- Feed, bathe, change and play with your baby.

1 to 3 Years
- Acts shy, clings to other parent/caregiver
- Hides, slow to come to you
- Does not recognize you, afraid of you
- Cries, has temper tantrums
- Regresses to earlier behavior (sucking thumb, trouble with toilet training)

How to Respond:
- Go slowly.
- Let the child set the pace.
- Don't force holding, hugging, kissing.
- Be gentle and fun; get involved with their play activities.
- Sit at their level.
- Make time for your child.
- Go easy on discipline for a while.

3 to 5 Years
- Feels scared or guilty/responsible for the separation (Parent left because he/she no longer cares about me, or I was bad.)
- Feels abandoned
- Tests limits

How to Respond:
- Accept the child's feelings.
- Focus on rewarding desirable behaviors.
- Talk to child about his/her interests.

- Support the other parent/caregiver when they enforce family rules.
- Go easy on the discipline for a while.
- Make time for the child.
- Participate in their play activities; what do they enjoy doing? (Games, drawing, clay, books, etc.)

5 to 12 Years
- Worries about how their role in the family may change
- Anger
- Boys feel competition with Dad for masculine role
- Torn by loyalties to parent/caregiver who stayed behind
- If relationship was good before separation:
    Very excited, proud
    Happy to see parent
    Wants to monopolize returning parent's time and attention
- If relationship had problems before separation:
    Fears parent's return
    Withdrawn and hesitant

How to Respond:
- Give lots of attention.
- Review photos, school work, activities, etc., with child.
- Praise what they have accomplished while you were gone.
- Avoid criticism and unnecessary discipline.
- Show interest in feelings, activities, accomplishments, and dreams by listening carefully. (New toys, new friends, new teacher, books read, school, etc.)
- Spend time alone with them doing something they like to do.
- Help them understand what you did while gone.

13 to 18 Years

- Mixed feelings about your return
- Excited about your return, relieved
- Withdrawn, angry, resentful
- Wonders how household will change after your return
- Feels self-conscious about expressing feelings
- Mood swings
- Tries to act "cool" in front of peers; acts as if he/she doesn't care

How to Respond:

- Praise what they have accomplished while you were gone.
- Tell them how important they are and how glad you are that they helped the family.
- Don't criticize or tease—teens can be very sensitive.
- Make time to talk about what is new in his/her life and how he/she is feeling.
- Give them your undivided attention.
- Try to understand; see through their eyes.
- Don't judge.
- Ask for their input before changing household rules.
- Respect routines they have established while you were gone.
- Respect their privacy.
- Ask about what was hard and what was easy while you were gone.
- They need to be seen and heard. This helps them feel appreciated and respected.
- Share some of your deployment experiences with him/her as appropriate. (Do these things even if they are withdrawn and/or act like they don't care.)

If you're the spouse who remained at home, realize that you may have to act as a "buffer" between your husband or wife and other children around the neighborhood. You can run interference to better help your spouse feel comfortable in answering children's prying questions.

Since reunion starts from the time you tell the family that the servicemember is coming home, I did rely on the advice of child and family counselors to answer the question, "When should we tell the kids?" I was told the classic answer, "It depends." And it does. It depends primarily on their age and maturity. Here's a summary of their advice:

- For those young ones who are still at home and haven't entered school, you should tell them closer to when the parent is actually coming home. This makes sense because little ones don't have a very good sense of time. Remember when you did the counting jar or taking a link off a paper chain for each day they were gone? That's the reason those ideas worked so well—the child could only understand what was happening that day and could visually see the "count down" as links were removed. They'll be fine with you saying something like, "Daddy will be home after you go to sleep and wake up two more times." They may not be able to process much more than that.

- School age children know more about time. That may have to do with the idea that they relate things now to their school day. It occurs to me that my earliest memories of growing up began when I started school. You can provide more details at this age and give them more of a "lead time." That will let them take part in the planning activities for homecoming like making banners, shopping for favorite foods, etc. This also gives more time to answer questions that arise. A bit more time lets a child think things out and do their own planning and preparing.

- What about teenagers? My first reaction is that they tend to tune things out. When I asked about this, I was told that it is true that teens can become even moodier and more stand-offish than they usually are! Remember, you won't be disappointed if that's what you expect. As the parent at home, read the signals from your teen as to when you should let them in on the news. Then you can keep them up to date on the details as the time gets closer. From this point on, you may have to just "let them be" and adjust on their own. Always let them know that you're here to talk if they want to. Some will and others won't. I hear from parents that it depends a lot on the type of relationship you've had all along and what you've each come to expect as far as predictable behavior.

You know I'm not a psychologist, so as I share the ideas that others have sent to me, know that if in your own situation things are not progressing as you think they should, don't hesitate to seek the advice of a professional. Utilize the support groups, friends, counselors and chaplains around you. Many have gone through the same experiences and can shed some light for you. I'll continue to include their advice along with that of the military families I interviewed.

125 Be observant to changes in behavior. You need clues as to what's going on, especially with those pesky "pre-teen" ages. Think about three or four ways that you've been able to tell if your child is stressed, depressed or mad in the past. You might want to write these down. Then if you see these signals, you can talk as parent/child and see if you can find out what's causing these feelings. If you do see the signs, don't ignore them.

126 I've combined two thoughts here. First Jennie said, "I think young teens have a difficult time adjusting. They change a great deal and take on quite a bit during deployments." Based on these comments from Jennie, I liked the idea that my office assistant, Jenn, came up with. "I never asked my thirteen-year-old to be the 'man of the house.' Instead I asked him to be the 'best thirteen-year-old' he could be. This helped him reach that goal without adding the pressure of adult responsibility to his teenage life. As a result, Sam really stepped up and took over some things that he knew he could do, including helping his little brother. It worked out even better than I expected!"

I'm not finished with the comments from Jennie. She went on to say that just as they start getting to know other military children, it ends due to the changing of units and less time to get together. Maybe the youth program could do more things following deployments that would help them to stay connected with other military kids. Jennie was referring to the youth programs that are part of the State Family Readiness Conferences held once a year in most states. Does your state have a conference? If so, why don't you approach them about adding a program for post deployment that will help these young people stay connected and utilize each other for continued support. Take time to still see your "battle buddies" even if it's for a short visit.

127 As a serviceperson, you might be worried about the ways you've changed while you've been gone. Guess what? Your children are feeling the same way. They might be afraid that you won't like what you see in them as they've grown. For example: new haircuts, clothing styles, and attitudes. Children should talk about these concerns before the reunion.

128 It's amazing what little kids rely on to connect to who their dad or mom is. Ashley said that Logan tells her he wants his "Daddy song" (which is "American Soldier" by Toby Keith) whenever he wants to see his daddy. It has constantly helped him know who Daddy is, so there is a greater connection when he comes home.

129 Before the deployed servicemember returns, help your children make a "My Daddy (Mommy) Box." Take a box (like a shoebox) and let them decorate the outside. Then they fill it with anything they want to show the returning parent. For example: school papers, pictures, thoughts, awards, etc. Then when the parent returns, they make their special time to sit down and go through the box. Each child does his/her own so they are truly personal.

130 Create a book of coupons for redemption upon the parent's return. Some suggestions:

- For kids: movie with Mom or Dad; candy bar of your choice; Dairy Queen® trip; making their favorite dinner; out to their favorite restaurant; etc.

- For spouse: time together; hugs and kisses (or more); favorite romantic dinner; doing one of the spouse's chores around the house; etc.

131 Start now to create a journal of entries entitled "The most important thing I learned today." Compile these lessons and give the book of knowledge to your child upon graduation from high school. It will always go with him/her as a foundation for whatever avenue he/she chooses to take.

132 Share yourself with your school-age children. Discuss some of what it was like to be deployed. Be an integral part of what's going on in their lives. Write notes of encouragement for a project or activity they're doing in school. Put the notes in their lunch boxes or on their pillows at night. Start with shorter notes for younger children and then you can get more involved as they grow older.

There's no greater gift than the giving of yourself and your time. I love hearing ideas that involve how families use their personal time together to forge new bonds.

133 Chaplain Stroud, USAF (Retired) shares, "How can kids feel close to their dad who is on the other side of the world when he has no access to the internet and can only afford to call home twice a month? That was the dilemma our family faced back in the eighties, before the internet was a gleam in the global eye. Knowing that Aaron, Kristen and Lucas would only hear my voice two times a month troubled me, and I came up with an idea I'd never heard proposed up to the day I received my orders for a yearlong 'remote.' I would record some very special books on cassette tapes (today a person can do it digitally). My children could listen to them whenever they wanted. As a Christian chaplain it should come as no surprise that I chose *The Chronicles of Narnia*. Hearing Dad's voice every day (they literally wore the tapes out) made my kids feel like I had been 'not so far away' that entire year. I encourage others who are facing lengthy deployments or unaccompanied tours to consider recording some worthwhile literature for their kids. Even with today's cheaper calling rates and instantaneous emails, these personal story-times can build very precious memories."

The reason I shared Chaplain Stroud's "during" deployment idea is because I believe that the constant hearing of the deployed person's voice keeps a bond strong, which makes it easier to reconnect. The distance doesn't seem as far; the time doesn't seem as long. It's also a great idea to keep your kids exposed to, as he put it, "worthwhile literature." You need something to offset the amount of violence and anger kids see every day.

134 What a pleasure to hear from the dads who are deployed about what's important to them. Jim, thank you for sharing this: "DAD'S DATE! Teenagers often feel left out of the homecoming. One (especially for daughters) is to create a bond. This is where dad and daughter (or MOM'S DATE with mother and son for deployed moms) go to a nice place to eat— maybe a coat and tie type of place for fine dining. Beforehand, Dad or Mom writes a letter about his or her feelings about life. This must be a handwritten letter. Then talk about the letter and what the deployment meant to both of them. At the end of the meal Dad can give his daughter a music box to keep the letter in. I have many different ways to use "Dad's Date." Girls go through many changes while Dad is gone; he might leave his little girl and come home to a young lady! Dad's dates helps them both. Same for moms and sons." The greatest gift you can give your children is to love their parents.

135 Chris added onto this by saying that the one-on-one time he had with each child was beneficial for his whole family upon his return. This is a reminder to distribute your time as evenly as you can if you have more than one child in your family.

One of my son's friends had "date night" with her dad, too. Their favorite activity was going to play miniature golf and then off to Dairy Queen® for an ice cream cone dipped in chocolate!

136 "During my service in Afghanistan, my fiancé (now wife) sent me an email every day. She is a middle school teacher and she sent me questions that her students had. This allowed me to share information about questions that she and others had and gave her a better idea of what I was experiencing. I also have a daughter who was in the first and second grades while I was deployed. We kept in touch via email and satellite phone. When I came home, I was a 'show and tell' item at her school! Just as in the emails to the middle school class, this let the kids in my daughter's class ask questions."

137 Here's an amazingly simple and fun way to spend a little time together as a family. "When my husband came home, we went to one new place a day. Some were new businesses, shops, parks or someplace I found while he was gone." The best part is experiencing these together.

Along these same lines, my husband, Larry, and I planned a driving vacation. We had an "ending point" which was to arrive in Michigan on a certain date to attend my niece's graduation. We had two weeks to get there. The design of the entire trip was that everything we did and every place we ate and stayed was someplace we had never been before. So in South Dakota we saw the National Woodworkers Museum (who knew) and toured that. We took a train for the first time and saw Mt. Rushmore on our way down to the Mall of America (nope, never been there) in Minnesota. It was not only fun to see and do new things, but great that we were seeing and doing them for the first time together. Maybe this would be a nice way to pretend that things are new and wonderful for you, too.

138 Kathleen Edick, co-author with Paula Johnson of the wonderful children's book *We Serve Too!* and their new book *We Serve Too! 2*, suggests that "If the deployed parent can save some of the letters, photos or drawings that the children made and sent to the parent while deployed, and then show them to the child when they return, the child will feel that his or her efforts have made a difference. When the inevitable comes about and the conversation goes to the events that the parent was not there for, the parent has evidence that the connection has been made even from far away. Example: "Yes, I did miss you at Christmas, but you sent me this letter and it sure meant a lot to me," or "I know I was not here for your birthday, but see the photos you sent? I looked at them and thought of you."

---◆---

**You can find more information about both
We Serve Too and *We Serve Too, 2*
at *www.weservetoo.com* including
how to get copies for yourself and
the families you work with.**

---◆---

139 "When I deployed, the first thing I bought and mailed to my kids was a t-shirt from the operation or country I was in. This allowed them to wear it during my deployment and made teachers, youth leaders, etc. aware of my absence. They also wore the shirts when they met me when I got home." – Deb

140 Since in some branches of service TDYs are shorter but more frequent, it helps the coming-home phase when kids are too young to feel a sense of distance or time. This idea relates to the period of time during deployment, but I really like it because it's part of what makes the return better. Autumn said, "When my toddlers ask, 'Where's Papa?,' I reply, 'He's at work far away.'" She says that it doesn't seem so much like "forever" this way.

"But Dad said I could!"—Tackling discipline while maintaining a united front . . .

So your kids aren't the little angels that you expected them to be when you walked in the door? Give your expectations a reality check—or borrow some well behaved kids!

When I was growing up we loved birthday celebrations! When it was your birthday, it was your day. You picked the meal *you* wanted and even what kind of cake you wanted, so of course we always saw birthdays as special and fun, with one exception. When I think back on my mother's birthdays I remember her crying. It just seemed like she would be mad at us during the day, and by the time cake came, she was pretty much in tears. I didn't think we were that bad, but I guessed we must have been. How awful to be the reason for causing tears on Mom's special day. (In reality, she probably didn't cry every year, but it sure seemed like it.)

Years later, when Mom and I talked about those times, here's what she said, "I think it was my own fault that I ended up crying. I raised four normal kids and you all did your share of fighting with each other. For some reason, when my birthday rolled around I expected the four of you to miraculously become little angels and not fight or argue. I expected you to change from who you were all year, and when you didn't, I got upset. You didn't behave in any way differently on that day than you did all year, so I learned to change my expectations. I knew that I had four great normal kids—what more could I want?"

One of the challenges I hear a lot is a deployed parent trying to step right back in and discipline the children. This causes confusion because the kids have abided by one parent's rules for so long, and now someone new steps in and attempts to pick up where he or she left off. Then you're left to wonder why everyone's rebelling. Just like with my mother, know what your expectations are and then discuss them with the parent who's been handling things all along. Communication remains the constant thread throughout this time, too. Please be sure that everyone knows what's expected of them. One woman wrote that along with communication, you need to get confirmation from the other parent as you begin to resume discipline roles. **Be sure that you're not disciplining behavior that was "allowed" during your absence.**

Help children to know their limits, especially those who are about ten to fifteen years old. For 37 years my husband, Larry, was a middle school math teacher. He told me what would happen every September with a new class. He always knew that they would "push the barriers" of what they could get away with and "test their (and your) limits." Larry knew that they would have to see what they could get away with—almost like it was expected of them. But the ironic thing was that they really did want controls and guidelines, even when they acted as if they wanted to get away with everything. Kids really don't know how to act without parameters and boundaries to their behavior. Within that first week, they knew what they could get away with and what they couldn't. Yes, it's confusing, but they're kids. That's their job! Give your own kids time to discover the new parameters now that you're home.

141 Kathleen writes, "In our new book on reunion, the father says to the child, 'Respect is the glue that keeps us together.' Don't be afraid to pick up the authority necessary to be a parent. It has been a long time, and you want the kids to be happy you're home. The truth is, however, they need to know that you are the parent. It is comforting to children to know who is in charge and to say out loud that yes, the other parent has been in charge, but you're the parent too, and you're home now. It will take some time for everyone to get used to the changes, but they are good changes and you will be fine."

I find that at about this time Mom is at a burnout level; so Dad, stay tuned in to what discipline is needed and begin to "blend" in.

142 Realize that when a child really is upset or emotionally holding things in, you might just need to let them express themselves in their own way. For some kids, they find that they can express themselves through art. If they like to draw or paint, then let them. Afterward, you can talk to them about their artwork. That might give you an eye into what they are feeling.

143 "Coming home can be a bit of a 'culture shock.' The deployed parent may have been in very stressful situations while he was gone in wartime. Home is unfamiliar. He may not want to drive for a little while. Usually when my husband gets back he just wants to sit back and 'observe,' which is the best thing for him to do. I can kind of show him how it's been working while he's been gone, and he doesn't have the responsibility to 'jump right in' and try to make up for the last fifteen months he's been gone. Honestly, at first I don't want him to jump in and start disciplining our son. Yes, he may be his child, but I was all he had for the entire time Dad was gone. He needs to watch how I work with our son, and I need to see his response to how he reacts toward him.

In our situation, which may be the same for lots of people, our little guy was almost two when his dad left, and now when he returns (next week) our son will be two weeks from turning three. What a difference that is to a parent and a child. When Dad left, our son wasn't even really talking. When he gets back, our son will be saying sentences. Remember, your spouse will need time to adjust to his child, too. Even if your child/chidren are not this young, everyone has changed during this time, and we need that time to get to know each other slowly. Don't overwhelm your spouse by trying to 'catch up' (with chores or life in general) from a fifteen-month deployment in just one day!"

144 "Remember that older kids change, too. They took on responsibility that they didn't have before. Our thirteen-year-old grew five inches in that year! He really was an entirely different person when Mike returned." – Jenn

Are you returning as a single parent? . . .

There is an amazing amount of joy in coming back and giving your child a huge hug. The challenge, as a single parent who was, up until the deployment, your child's most influential parent, is realizing that someone else took care of your youngster. That person had the responsibility for discipline and the fun of being a part of your child's daily activities. Someone else was there to help with the homework, and at first you might feel pangs of jealously over the bond that your child will have formed with his/her temporary caregiver. You're probably thinking that this concern just isn't "fair" because after all, the caregiver was most likely a grandparent, very close friend, or other family member. You know what? You're normal! It's hard knowing that someone else was there for the cuts and scrapes, the baseball games and nightly homework help. (Unless you're terrible in math like I am, and then you welcome the homework help!)

There is an adjustment to be made and you all are in it together. You'll find that many of the reconnection suggestions that are in the **Children and Reunion** section will be applicable for you, too. The biggest thing to remember is that your reconnection might take a bit more time. Please be patient as this period of transition can last for a few weeks. It will work out just fine if you keep communication open among all parties. Here are some tips:

145 Be grateful that your child or children had someone who cared enough for your family to step in and provide what you were temporarily unable to. They are the people who helped you maintain a connection with your kids from far away. Your children naturally needed someone to love and help them, and the smiles that they have for you now are because of that care. Tricia writes a reminder that "whatever you do, don't forget to say thank you in some way. Find a special gift that can be given from both you and those young ones they cared for."

146 This idea applies to ALL parents, not just those who are single. Sit down with your children and talk to them about what things were like during your absence. This period of readjustment is going to be different for them, too. There may have been different household rules, time schedules and traditions that they became used to. What of those changes would you as a family like to keep in force, and which ones are ready to be done away with? If you involve them in the changes, they will feel a sense of responsibility during a time when they might otherwise feel out of control. If they were living in a caregiver's home instead of their own during this time, you can imagine that "going home" is a big change for them, too. If you're in it together, you can make the transition a smooth one.

Even though I realize that it's not the same, an example of this idea comes to mind. My brother and his wife have fifteen- and eighteen-year-old sons. A couple of months ago the foundation of their house collapsed. They were displaced and had to live elsewhere during the reconstruction. My brother, Brad, and fifteen-year-old Patrick went to live with my mother; his wife went to stay with her mother; and the eighteen-year-old went to college. During these months, Patrick discovered that he liked it when his grandmother made dinner and they could all eat together. Their regular household routine is so busy with kids' activities that it left few times when they could eat together. Up until that time, Patrick didn't think that it mattered very much. That's different now, and he told his dad that when they are back together in their house, he'd like to make it more of a practice to have dinners together.

Times do change, and so do people. There might be a "new" tradition or routine that they've experienced that can now be a part of your home even when it wasn't in the past.

147 Now sit down and have a "heart-to-heart" with the caregiver. Learn all you can about any changes your children have gone through so they won't be a surprise. Find out how rules were enforced and what type of schedules they had. Were there behavior challenges to be dealt with? Do the children have any new friends you should know about? What are the other things that you "just should know" as their parent?

148 Whenever possible try to keep the caregiver involved in some way in your lives so that the separation isn't overly traumatic on anyone, including the caregiver. Joyce shared, "If the caregiver lives in your area, be sure that they have current sports and school activities schedules so they can come to a football game or science fair if they'd like. If the person lives farther away, be sure the kids remember birthdays, send occasional notes, and keep the caregiver in the loop through pictures." The internet is so great for this. Older children love to use their skills to create "a day in the life of" photo slideshows to be emailed.

You're going to do great! Remember to take it one day at a time.

A bit about "blended" families—Life in the mixer . . .

I'm part of a blended family. When Larry and I married he had two sons I had to make a part of our new family. I understand this because it was not easy. They were almost teenagers, and I figured that I'd have the chance to grow to love them before I got hit with the teen years! With a new baby added to the mix, it was more of a trial by fire. It all worked out, but not without its share of comments like, "You're not my mother," and "You can't tell me what to do."

At one point in my research, I put out there the question of how to keep blended families connected and working. I know that there are many families who fall into this category, but I was surprised by the few responses I received to this specific issue. I'm going to share what I did get back, and would like to keep the avenue on this open. If you're reading this because you're a blended family, please continue to send me your input in the comments section of www.ImAlreadyHome.com. I'll provide ongoing information in newsletters so we can get better at this. Here are some of the situations people found themselves in and maybe you can identify.

- "In my case, my husband had to have a conference call with a judge here in the states to grant me time with my stepchildren."

- "My husband was deployed to Kuwait. My nine-year-old stepdaughter was not allowed to communicate with me due to her mother's dislike of me. I decided to stay in touch with her (one-way communication) by sending pictures I got of her dad's deployment including his Welcome Home."

- "My husband's ex-wife started with the phone calls, fighting over time spent with the kids, etc., the minute he got home. I would have liked a little breather."

It hurts me to hear that the adults can't get along. How do you expect the kids to? I wish you'd try to keep an open mind and treat all your communications with each other in the manner that most benefits them. Of the responses I did get regarding blended families, I liked this letter best. I'm sharing the entire thing:

Dear Elaine,

My husband and I are both stepparents and in the National Guard. Also, my ex is in the Guard and has been to Iraq twice. There is no question that this situation is hard. The best thing that my husband and I have found that works is absolute, concrete firmness about "The Family." We make sure that whenever we have the kiddies at our home, that it is their home. We try our level best to ensure that the kids know that our home is HOME. There are no "stepkids" and "stepparents." Everyone has a place and belongs. We try to act like a normal family as much as possible. We eat dinner together and everyone gets to discuss their day one at a time. We do lots of family things together. My brothers are his kids' uncles just as much as they are my kids' uncles and vice versa with his sister and my kids. My mom is grandmother to everyone. I think that this is the basis for communication. The kids want to communicate.

149 I went to Germany recently and whenever I called home my husband made sure that I spoke with every child. I treat them all like my own, even when they don't like it. My husband made sure that they all had a chance to email me also.

150 I bought postcards and mailed them to the kids' classrooms. They LOVED that! The teacher allowed them to read it to the class or if they were too young, she read it for them. I addressed the postcard to the class and not just to my child. I also mailed each of the children a postcard to our home so they could receive mail just from me.

151 The kids kept a box of all their art and great school papers to show me when I got home. You can decorate this box with pictures of you and them. Do it together ahead of time.

152 Before I left, I made sure to give each child a picture of me and Daddy together and I tried to find one that had that child in it. Wedding pictures are great for that.

153 I sprayed my perfume on my t-shirts and gave each child a shirt. My seven-year-old stepson threw a fit one day because they started to leave for school and he forgot my shirt in his bed. My husband had to go back in the house and get it. My stepson slept with it and took it everywhere he went.

Those are just a few things that we did, but I can't emphasize enough that it begins with good communication in the home and not acting like a blended family. As much as possible, act like a normal family from discipline to making family memories.

◆───────────

A good book to read is
Disciplines of a Godly Family
by R. Kent Hughes and Barbara Hughes.
This book helps with creating that
family stability.
You can find it at _Amazon.com_.

───────────◆

Be Blessed!

To close this section, it's my pleasure to share part of an email I received from Tim in the Navy who is frequently sent out on six-month assignments. He gave me permission to share his thoughts and it's the perfect "smile" we need here.

"Now let me let you in on my version of David Letterman's Number 1. Drum roll please! The Number 1 thing about a six-month deployment is when the ship pulls back into port and I see the faces of my wife and daughters. There is no room for being too proud to be a man; the tears just roll. That first hug and kiss after six months! There is nothing to compare. The pain, agony, negative emotions, and worrying ALL disappear in one moment as I sweep all three of them up in my arms. That's what makes it worth it and that's what gets you through it."

Tim, I don't know anyone who could have summed it up better. Thank you.

Chapter 3
The Unspoken Side of Reunion

The Unspoken Side of Reunion

◆ ◆ ◆

"I didn't sign up for this."

This is where "the rubber meets the road," as is often said. This is the section of the book that has been so difficult to write. You remember early on I referred to a quote that came from an Army wife who reminded me that "reunion isn't all balloons and parties." She was absolutely right. While many servicemembers are able to return and reintegrate fairly comfortably with their families and communities, many are not. We, as civilians, hear the casualty count from the war and grieve for the families, but what we don't hear are the numbers for those who are MEDEVAC'ed with injuries to Walter Reed Hospital, are plagued with mental issues ranging from combat stress to Post Traumatic Stress Disorder (PTSD), and those with Traumatic Brain Injuries (TBI). We cannot talk about reunion and its effect on families without spending some time helping with these issues.

This seems to be a good place for a disclaimer. You know that my purpose in writing is not to present a problem or situation without also presenting some solutions or coping mechanisms that others have shared. I am far from being an expert in the areas we're going to address here, and I do not profess to be. There are so many others who are. What I can do is bring you information gleaned from many indepth conversations and the understanding of what can be done. I find it best to bring you some of the stories I've heard, the "discovery points" from each, and weave in the advice from experts. My thought is that you might be able to identify with a story or situation and realize that others are going through it too. There's nothing better to show you that you really are normal and there are roads for you to take.

Post Traumatic Stress Disorder

"Mental health is indispensable to personal well-being, family and interpersonal relationships, and contribution to community or society."
– Department of Defense, 2007

Let's start here because some form of PTSD, from mild combat stress to severe, affects many servicemembers following combat. I had the privilege of speaking with Lawrence Luck who, among so many others, has been a medic dealing with PTSD for over twenty years. Please read his full list of expertise, along with his contact information in the back of this book. He asked if he could share his thoughts and insight as he talks about combat stress and PTSD.

Laying a Foundation of Understanding
by Lawrence Luck

When we talk about combat stress and PTSD, the first realization hits. That is that the person who deployed is no longer the exact same person returning home. Depending on the amount of action the individual participated in, or was an ongoing active part of, it will require every bit of compassion, understanding and long-term devotion you can muster. Guilt, survivor's remorse, self denial and activities he/she was required to perform for the mission will forever be a reoccurring nightmare (day or night) for these individuals.

Their age and level of preparedness will also play a large role in how well the individual copes with the memories. Many will not seek help due to the fear of being stigmatized by having sought assistance.

———————◆———————

This is where MilitaryOneSource's Wounded Warrior Resource Center is helpful. Find it at their interactive website: *www.MilitaryOneSource.com* or call 1-800-342-9647.

———————◆———————

Others refuse to believe that they need help dealing with the recurring memories and daytime visions. All feel a depression of some state without knowing that they are depressed. Resumption of old activities may no longer hold any pleasure for them. Intimacy can be an issue that also falters. The inability to perform and gratify their loved one will provoke a wide variety of emotions that can be self-destructive as well as self-punishing. A total commitment to the individual requires tolerance for things you do not understand, and you probably never will.

When he/she speaks of the emotional attachment to the men and women they served with, DO NOT cast off this attachment as unnecessary or unnatural. No amount of academic learning can compare to having lived the event. Patronizing the individual will only cause further distancing from you, and you will surely lose the battle. Listen, love, be faithful and remember not only are you relearning your loved one, but they are having to relearn coping with a society as fickle as they are indecisive about their commitment to the men and women serving.

154 Immediately upon them returning home, don't talk about battle or incursions; don't talk about the servicemembers who were lost, or how they died. DO be a good and attentive listener, and do not give lame lines on when YOU think they should be over their mourning of lost friends. Their readjustment is as much a process of mourning a loss of time with family, personal achievements and goals, and an extreme loss of self and who they feel they should be. A unique dynamic is in play and will have to wind itself down in order for the individual to grasp a sense of personal control.

Relationships can sometimes end due to the partner's inability to cope with the abrupt devastation that returns with them. Anger, rage, and a sense of loss or betrayal is what fuels these emotions. Remember that this may just be the tip of the iceberg. A great number of service persons return home wounded or disabled and this is compounded by the fact that many of them are very young. Emotional abandonment is the greatest fear of all, along with the fear of not being wanted by their loved ones because of their wounds. Yet they still require love, support, and the knowledge that no matter what part of them is no longer their own, that they are loved simply for being themselves and who they are— not for what they did.

Do you recognize some of yourself or your service-member in the above? I don't want to leave you with the idea that hope is far away. On the contrary; there are things you can do for and with your loved one to help straddle the space between the hurt and getting on with a wonderful life.

155 Assist them in beginning a journal to write down things that they do not openly want to talk about but they want to acknowledge in their minds. It is an outlet that is theirs and theirs alone.

Never ask what the content of the journal is, and provide them the space to readjust.

156 Know that certain sights, sounds, and odors will always trigger some response—negative or positive—and just because they do not appear to be reacting openly, passive anxiety attaché can still be present. Be aware of subtle changes in emotional responses, both verbal and physical. Some might include, but not be limited to, clenched fists when they get frustrated, gritting of teeth, heavy breathing, and a difference in their overall standing posture.

157 Maintain a calm, soothing voice to reassure them that they are in a safe place . . . home.

158 When they are sleeping, do not actively touch them if they are experiencing a nightmare.

159 Talk to the individual's friends he or she served with and listen not only to what they say but to how they say it. This will help you tune in to important details and hopefully help you better understand their reactions to particular situations. For example, why they no longer like banana pudding. You find out that the reason is that while they were at chow and eating banana pudding, an IED went off at the end of the chow hall and killed three of his buddies. Every time he smells or sees banana pudding it reminds him of his friends and that tragic event. If you hadn't talked with his friends, you may never have known this.

Please know that in this seemingly depressing scenario, there are most certainly rays of hope. Most people will recover in time with total devotion from loved ones, those around them who care, and professional resources.

160 Be sure that both you and your service-member maintain contact with support groups and individuals. Network with them on what to expect and how to cope with the day-to-day uncertainty; believe me, there will be day-to-day uncertainty. Keep the faith, and seek whatever help you need to gain a better understanding of what is going on in your life after your loved one returns.

Thank you, Larry.

Following up on this foundation, we hear from Lynda who writes, "Please note the very significant difference between combat stress and PTSD. Everyone comes back with a form of combat stress; not everyone has PTSD. I'd like to share a great website with your readers:

---◆---

www.Battlemind.org/spouse
**will help military spouses understand their
Soldier/Marine/Airman/Sailor better and
help them through the transition from
combat to home.**

---◆---

161 With regard to PTSD, Dawn writes, "A soldier may not tell you what he/she has encountered. Be patient. Encourage the soldier to seek help but don't force the soldier into professional care. Don't avoid the *battle buddies*; they all share similar experiences to those of your soldier. Know the signs: isolation, forgetfulness, sleepless nights, nightmares, depression, always on 'alert,' etc."

◆

**The best resource I've found
is _www.NMHA.org_.
Type in Post Traumatic Stress Disorder
in the search engine.
There are numerous links for research.**

◆

I value the insights of the professionals I've invited to share in all my books. In _I'm Already Home . . . Again_ I began to address the trials of reunion by bringing an article written by Linda Engelman who holds a Master's degree in clinical counseling and is the lead instructor for the CISM sponsored Trained Crisis Responder course in North Dakota. I should also mention that she has been married to a National Guardsman for 37 years and served as her state's Lead Volunteer. In my eyes, that gives Linda the right to share this information.

You might want to bookmark this page for reference often. Here's what Linda's experience can bring to you:

Reunion: Prospect and Possibility
by Linda Engelman

As you look to reunion you probably hope that life will soon return to normal. You have been told that weathering a lengthy, dangerous deployment will change you, creating a "new" normal. But many of you have no previous experience on which to predict your responses. Therefore, with the anticipation can come some uneasiness.

Because knowledge eases anxieties and helps put things in perspective, I've been invited to provide some information about reunion and Post-traumatic Stress.

It is not only common for military members to experience Post-traumatic Stress, it is expected. A normal response to an abnormal situation, reunion is a time of readjustment, a time of transition—literally from one world to another—for your military member.

For family members it is a time for reintegration, a time for opening the family boundaries to make room for the returning veteran. This is both exciting and stressful for everyone. So while I will focus specifically on the military member, know that the whole family can be at risk.

What are some common PTS responses?

Military members often report the following:

1. Feeling flat, apathetic and lethargic. Living under constant threat and with all the other irritants results in high levels of hormone (like adrenaline) production. Coming home, as adrenaline levels go down, the lack of stimulation can result in depression.

2. Feeling isolated and lonely. One young soldier said that in Iraq, if she had a problem or concern, there was always somebody to talk with. Now there isn't that constant availability.

3. Feeling guilty. "I should be in Iraq helping," or "Why did I survive and my buddy die?"

4. Feeling on edge. Called the hyper-startle reflex, it takes a while to quit looking for an M16, to quit flinching at sudden sounds, to relax when noticing debris by the road, etc.

5. Feeling like they don't fit in and experiencing grief over the losses, including missing their military family in Iraq. Families report finding their

military member staring out the window for long periods or going for car rides alone. Following such a dramatic and life-altering experience, it takes time to completely come home.

6. Additionally, common responses include:
   - Difficulty concentrating
   - Preoccupation with the event
   - Anxiety, mood swings, headaches
   - Anger, fear, phobic avoidance
   - Loss of appetite and/or energy
   - Sleeping too much or too little
   - Self-medication, often with alcohol
   - Withdrawal from church or anger at God
   - Family discord, arguing, crying
   - Reoccurring dreams
   - Risk-taking behavior

When should we think about talking with a professional?

While it is common for symptoms to appear at any time, frequently they start three to six months after returning—when the honeymoon period is over.

Always consult a professional if symptoms don't diminish significantly within 30 days. And always consult a professional if symptoms are dangerous or debilitating.

Finding a therapeutic listener can insure that this experience is integrated into the fabric of your life, rather than defining your whole life. Looking to the veterans of previous wars, we know that folks can live well and have long, fulfilling, productive lives. Doing the right things today can make ALL the difference!

How can I find a professional?

There are a number of ways to access help:

1. Call your Family Assistance Center or Family Program Office for a referral. Be sure to ask about the free counseling sessions available through One Source to veterans and their families.

2. Call your family physician.

3. Ask your military chaplain or civilian minister.

4. Go to your local Veterans Center.

(**Author's note:** You will also find assistance at www.militaryonesource.com.)

If the first person you talk to isn't helpful, don't give up! Be persistent and try another. As in other traumatic times, it is not advisable to make major life-changing decisions for at least a year. In the end, this experience can strengthen you and add depth and substance to your life. It is full of prospect and possibility!

You can read more about Linda in the **Permissions** section at the back of this book.

162 In a casual conversation we had, Linda gave me some specifics about her advice not to make major decisions in the first six months after returning home, whenever possible. Don't buy a new house or car, change jobs, or file for divorce. Too much readjustment occurs during these six months, and you may very well settle in and feel differently about the decision after that time.

163 Ashley always has amazing things to share with me, and I value being able to bring them to you. She sums up her advice here:

"Give your spouse space. Let him take time to soak it all up and take it all in. Let him go into another room if he feels overwhelmed with all that is going on. Although it is a great experience to be reunited, it is very stressful, too. You are trying to find your niche together again. It has been a long time since you have been a couple, and it takes a little while to get back into the groove. If it any time you feel your spouse's behavior has changed so much that he is showing signs of depression or suicidal thoughts, please talk to him and report it to the doctors. This can be PTSD. And please don't give up on getting him the help he needs. War is very traumatic, and this devastating disorder is not to be taken lightly."

I value the references to the stressors that contribute to different levels of PTSD and combat stress. Basic stressors are not to be taken in stride, nor should you look at only combat-related stress. A new study from the University of Michigan which looks at Air Force women who have deployed to Iraq found that about 20% of the 1,114 respondents suffer from at least one major symptom of PTSD. What interested researchers more is the fact that they were able to pinpoint work/family stress as "an independent and significant predictor of PTSD, above and beyond combat exposure," said Air Force Reserve nurse Col. Penny Pierce, an associate professor in the university's School of Nursing. Pierce, who is co-head of an ongoing study on deployment related stressors added, "This finding is important because there are things we can do to help minimize work/family stress."[2]

Col. Pierce is right. That's exactly why this guide and others like it are written. It's because when you're willing to take the time and apply a little creativity to an idea, you can make a positive effort to reduce the natural stress around your home and workplace. Many people call this "work/life balance." I found through a Google search that you can find many state- or community-specific seminars that deal with helping you to balance your life in a time when things can seem so overwhelming.

Another positive approach to helping servicemembers handle stress is a study that is currently being done at the time of printing. It's well known that bases and posts are bracing themselves for a surge in the number of psychological issues and problems among those returning primarily from Iraq and Afghanistan. It's been estimated that at least 63,000 active duty Army soldiers have served three or more tours. Many of the troops that are being followed are from the 101st Airborne combat brigades. Ft. Campbell is expanding their health-care providers to handle the surge. According to current information, they have nearly doubled their staff of psychologists and behavioral specialists. Army posts around the country are watching how things are handled at Ft. Campbell to see how army post's medical facilities will need to be ramped up to adequately meet the need[3].

The willingness of the Department of Defense to research ways to help with this transition, along with the enactment of the Yellow Ribbon legislation, shows me that our servicemembers and their families will be getting more than "lip service" to their concerns. Please use the myriad resources available around you in both the civilian and military communities.

One particular resource that was referred to me
is another book. Take a look at
*Tears of a Warrior: A Family's Story of
Combat and Living with PTSD*
by Janet J. Seahorn, Ph.D. and
E. Anthony Seahorn, MBA.
It's the first-hand experience of a
young army officer who served in Viet Nam
and the perspective of the wife and mother
who lived with a veteran suffering from PTSD.
For more information, please visit
www.TearsofaWarrior.com.

As we keep discovering, there are so many levels of
PTSD from combat stress to the more serious Traumatic
Brain Injury. I've learned things about TBI in the past
year or so, particularly how difficult it is to totally
understand!

As always, I'll bring you what I know in a way that I
believe will help you to gather some information, look
at some symptoms, and decide how to proceed from here.
I'll give you my sources and places to look for more
detail into your specific needs and questions.

A Short Look at Traumatic Brain Injury

Through my research I've found that there is often a thin line between recognizing the symptoms of PTSD and those of mild Traumatic Brain Injury (TBI). I also discovered that the information and resources out there to help with TBI are plentiful and way beyond my initial level of understanding. I decided to use a couple of my favorite resources to bring you some basic information from which you can identify an area of need, and then help you figure out how to learn more about your specific needs and questions. I'll tell you though, that this area of brain injury is something I can speak to based on personal experience. Maybe that is one reason why this section was difficult for me to write. You'll learn more about that later, and what I learned from it.

The handbook *Mild Traumatic Brain Injury: A Survivor's Handbook* by Theta Theta No Beta, defines Mild Traumatic Brain Injury (MTBI) as the "name given to head injuries where there is no open wound, but enough force to shake the brain inside the skull." They go on to say that "After such an injury, the way your brain processes information and communicates with your body is different from how it did prior to the accident, and may feel or seem interrupted. These brain interruptions can cause physical problems and affect your emotional well being, as well as your brain's ability to function."[4]

(Used with permission of the Brain Injury Hope Foundation.)

It would appear from the definition that one would know if they had suffered such an injury. But then things begin to get confusing, as they go on with their daily lives. Everything may seem "normal" at the onset, but then the injured person begins to have trouble with thoughts or tasks that were natural before the injury, and they begin exhibiting challenging behavior traits. They're soon asking themselves, "Is this really normal?"

Maybe the injured servicemember has now returned to the states and their family is noticing these same changes. How does one know when it's time to call for help? The authors of *Mild Traumatic Brain Injury: A Survivor's Handbook* have answered some of these questions in a clear and easily understandable way. I liked the checklist they printed that helped make an initial determination if help is needed. They've given permission for me to share that with you as a starting point.

Physical symptoms may include:

Headaches

Loss of balance

Vision problems

Dizziness

Loss of sex drive

Sleep disturbance

Loss of energy

Difficulty thinking of words

Easily fatigued

Sensitivity to light, sound or touch

Emotional symptoms may include:

Depression

Fearfulness

Apathy

Low motivation

Gullibility

Nightmares

Hyper vigilance and an exaggerated startle response

Mood swings and outbursts

Easily overloaded

Anxiety and frustration

Difficulty managing emotions

Sense of helplessness

Loss of sense of self, low self-esteem

Cognitive or thinking symptoms may include:

Memory loss

Short attention span

Slowed thinking

Disorientation

Brain fatigue

Forgetfulness

Difficulty driving

Inability to organize thoughts

Word finding and spelling difficulty

Impaired comprehension

Inability to make decisions

Medications can also cause or intensify some of these symptoms. Talk with your doctor to more fully understand any side affects your medication may cause.[5]

(Reprinted with permission from Mild Traumatic Brain Injury: A Survivor's Handbook.)

Personally, I found this handbook to be very useful. For example, the next chapter heading in the handbook is "What happened to my brain?" It doesn't get much clearer than that. The authors are currently working on an expanded and revised full book based on this handbook that is due to be released in spring 2009. If you would like more basic information, please get yourself a copy.

◆

*"Mild Traumatic Brain Injury (MTBI):
A Handbook of Hope for Our
Military Warriors and Their Families,"*
**by Mary Ann Keatley, Ph.D., Laura L. Whittemore
and Theta Theta No Beta Group.
Released by the
Brain Injury Hope Foundation.
Visit *www.BrainInjuryHopeFoundation.org*
for ordering information.**

◆

As mentioned earlier, many of the symptoms above parallel PTSD. You're probably thinking that it would be nice to know the next step in determining if the behavior is part of your family's new normal. There is a self assessment test you can find at www.BrainInjuryHopeFoundation.org and is a good place to begin because you're right there on the site and can find immediate answers to your questions. That's the first step in determining if further professional help is needed.

Another recommended resource is the Brain Injury Association of America at _www.biausa.org_.
There is even a link on the home page to brain injuries and the military.

This beginning piece can help you recognize if there is a need, and the above resources, along with those under "Mental and Physical Health" in the **Support** section of this book can begin to direct your search for assistance. Every person is different, so make your own discoveries, just as I did ten years ago. On March 26, 1999, my sister, then 44 years old, suffered a brain injury. Before I knew it, I was pacing in an Intensive Care Unit waiting room. The walls, supposedly painted to look soft and welcoming, instead felt cold and threatening. Random chairs sat scattered, while others formed small circles of comfort for families. This room was like no place else on earth. Time stood still here.

Rondi was in a coma, hooked up to life support and would remain that way for awhile. When she had finally stabilized enough to tolerate surgery she was given less than even odds of surviving, but she did. In the months that followed she underwent tests and retraining to help her gain back some of the life she had lost.

Looking back I remember something that started me thinking. During this time her marriage dissolved under the words, "You're not the woman I married." You know what? Truer words were never spoken. Throughout years of healing, she has been a single mom to two girls who also "lost" the mother they knew at the young ages of only five and seven. Everyone would have to get to know this "new" mother, daughter and sister.

As with any brain injury, healing goes on for years in one way or another. You all learn to live lives differently from what you had before. In our case, Rondi had been a teacher holding a Master's degree and now she was on permanent disability from work. It must have been devastating to know that she couldn't ever return to the work that had been her life for seventeen years. What was interesting, though, is that a few years ago she did return to a part time job, just not the one she had. She was able to renew a love she had for animals and learn a job that let her take care of them at a local pet shop. Her special attitude let her do this new job with the same dedication and love that she had for her prior position.

As with every story I tell, I send you off with tangible ideas or advice based on the experience. This is no different. As a family we learned some things that should help you to better understand some of what is happening to your loved one, or to someone else you might know. Here are your take-aways:

It's true, you are not the same person you were before the injury—at least not in the part of your brain that had suffered physical damage. The take-away from this is that it's okay, and now you have to begin to learn the new special parts of who you are with help from family and professionals. Rondi discovered that although she had lost much of her short-term memory, all of a sudden her long-term memory was extremely enhanced. We would listen to her recall parts of her early childhood and think, *How on earth did you ever remember that?!*

Don't be embarrassed to do what you have to do to make up for pieces you are missing. For example, when Rondi lost much of her short-term memory she decided that she always had to carry a small pad of paper and a pencil to write down anything anyone told her that she didn't want to forget. She knew her new weakness and had no problem asking people to repeat phone numbers, dates, or information while she wrote them down. She also made notes for herself of where she put things so she could find them later.

We learned that parts of the brain really do die when subjected to too much trauma. We could see on the x-ray that there was dark tissue in the middle of the brain. That small area wasn't functioning anymore and that was where she stored her ability to deal with finances and what are called "executive judgment skills." Knowing that this was physical helped because before that, when she would fail at something simple it was easy to snap at her and think that she just wasn't trying hard enough. Nothing could have been further from the truth. She was trying and was just as frustrated as we were. Advice: find out what those things are that can't be done for the moment, and find someone else to help out. In Rondi's case, my mother assumed control of her finances so she wouldn't go out and spend all her money.

Be patient. I feel like I say that over and over, but it's so hard to do! It's easy to get angry that the person you love is different, and it's scary to think that they may not be the same again. But don't take it out on them. Show as much patience as you can, and when it gets to be too much, go out and take a breather for a while. Remember, you have to take care of yourself, too.

We learned by working with the doctors that the brain can actually "rewire" itself to begin to perform those tasks that were lost in the damaged part. They call it "remapping" and in certain instances, when the brain discovers that it can no longer handle a task, it can eventually over time retrain another part of the brain to try to fill in. It doesn't happen all the time, and may not ever be a total recovery, but over time we've seen Rondi improve at skills that she wasn't able to do at all years ago.

One other suggestion that came from her adult daughter is, while a person is relearning tasks and retraining the brain, don't jump in and do everything that the person is having difficulty with. She said that at the beginning, Rondi would run hot water at the sink and her brain didn't recognize it as hot so Rondi would reach out to put her hands under the water. Her daughter would, out of instinct, grab her hands and pull them back so she wouldn't get hurt. In that instance, that wasn't necessarily the best thing to do because her brain needed to "feel" that it was hot and begin to recondition itself to know that hot water is dangerous. It's kind of like letting a small child learn what it feels like to fall off a chair so that in the future he won't stand on it. Of course, you wouldn't ever let your loved one be in a life threatening or dangerous situation, but if you can let them learn things for themselves, the brain will relearn it quicker, too.

Now, ten years later, Rondi continues to improve and we have all learned the concessions we need to make to compensate for the new person she is. What hasn't changed is that we still love her! I trust that you will see that your loved one gets the care he or she needs. As a family you can have the patience to see yourselves through this.

Our Wounded Warriors

Since fighting began in Afghanistan and Iraq, over 29,038 Americans have returned from a combat zone with physical wounds and a range of permanent disabilities including traumatic brain injury (TBI). Many more are struggling with less visible psychological injuries.[6] Welcoming home a wounded warrior is much different from being a part of the big, joint homecoming celebration. You are celebrating alone and in a different way. Erin Richardson has gone through this and talks about her experience so that it can help if you ever find yourself in this situation. She is very forthright and talks about this with such sincerity that with the exception of some changes for clarity of thought, I decided to present this as written.

Our Journey Began with a Phone Call
by Erin Richardson

I remember the call like it was yesterday, hearing that my husband, Matt, had been injured. He had only been deployed for a few months. A million emotions went through my head and I was at a loss for what to do; I felt completely helpless. I had been an Army wife for four years so I knew the Army worked as a process. It may not always make sense or seem practical, but the Army functions like it does for a reason. So the process of hearing about an injury begins when you receive the phone call, which serves as your notification. I was given the number for getting medical updates and advised that someone from the travel department would contact me so I could go to my husband. In the beginning I was given very little information about what happened because few details were available. Of course as the wife of an injured soldier, you want as much information as possible, but that doesn't speed the process.

The days following the initial "notification" phone call were filled with more phone calls, updates and arrangements. It seemed to take forever for Matt to get stateside. The waiting was frustrating because all I wanted to do was hop on a plane and get to my husband, but everyone I spoke to strongly advised me against that idea. Looking back it was so much easier to go with the Army's system, because they know what they are doing. Their systems have helped many other families be reunited as quickly and efficiently as possible after an injury. It is new to *you* but not to them.

164 While you wait for information to arrive, you have to plan for the time you will be away. You need a plan for your kids, your animals, your lawn care, your mail, paying bills and so many other things that will need attention. The list goes on and on. Looking back, these are the things that I could have planned for before Matt left. In hindsight, many of these details could have been prepared for way before the incident happened. Naming the support person ahead of time who I would call at a moment's notice would have saved me a lot of time and headache. If I had prepared my plan pre-deployment it would have been less stressful in those days immediately following Matt's incident.

165 I had no clue how long I would be away. I planned for a couple of weeks, but it ended up being about six months. If I had known then what

I know now, I would have packed a more versatile wardrobe. I especially would have packed a sweater and comfy shoes. You will probably be doing a lot of walking and hospital rooms can be chilly.

166 My son Ian was a little over a year old when Matt was injured. Initially I left him at home with my mom because I figured it would be easier on both of us if I could go and assess the situation first because I thought I would only be gone a few weeks. It turned out to be a decision I was very happy with. It allowed me to focus my energy on my husband without worrying about how Ian was being cared for. If at all possible I recommend having a family member or someone you trust look after your children.

When I was finally able to leave for Walter Reed Army Medical Center (WRAMC) to meet up with my husband, the Army arranged for someone in Washington, D.C. to pick me up and take me to the hospital. After arriving at WRAMC I was escorted to my husband and given a mini brief on the things I would have to do the next day. We all know it would not be the Army way without a brief. At that point I was just relieved that I had finally made it to my husband's side. All the stresses and worries that had bogged me down for the past few days were lifted. I knew he was here and alive. Whatever was yet to happen, and whatever the road ahead brought us, we could face it together. Just getting to the hospital felt like a huge relief. Of course that feeling was short lived because there is a ton of paperwork to fill out and things you have to do once you get there. There seemed to be a million visitors; doctors, social workers and anyone else you could think of were constantly in and out of Matt's room. Be prepared for nonstop activity.

167 I recommend that you bring a business card holder, because you will be given cards from lots of people. A related suggestion is to write something that will trigger your memory about that person on the back of each card because you will meet so many people and you can't remember everyone! Trust me, it's okay if you don't.

Through all this I realized how important family and friends are. I am not normally a person who likes help from anyone. I am independent and can handle anything and everything on my own. I realized that some things are too big to handle alone. My family and my husband's family were a big support system at a time when we needed it the most. Everyone wants to know what they can do to help, so let them. It may even help *them* more than it helps you because you've let them feel needed and useful.

168 Take time to digest everything. Your life will most likely not be the same and that's okay; you will eventually adjust to a new normal. At the time, I would not have wanted to hear, "Take it one day at a time," and here I am now passing it along to you! I had to figure that out for myself, and I wish someone had told me before this happened.

After I had been at WRAMC for about a month, I went home and got my son. That was a challenge because we had to figure out how to manage a VERY active thirteen-month-old. As you can imagine, a hospital is not a very fun spot for little kids, so you have to improvise.

169 We had special toys like a doctor's kit that he would play with while he sat with Dad in bed. Those were nice times. We had other toys that we left in the room that he could only play with while we were there. This made the toys seem more interesting since he couldn't take them along with us when we went "home" to bed. We also took lots of walks and explored. It's really trial and error, so figure out what works for you. WRMAC had a lot of things in place to help where possible. The hospital offers child care, BBQ's, concerts, and my favorite, famous visitors.

After almost six months we were able to finally come home. Once Matt was released from the hospital things got easier because we could do more and get out and about. The journey is not over. There are still a lot of new things we have to deal with and many uncertainties. It's a challenge to be on an active Army post where you don't really know where you fit because of the months of rehab Matt still needs to go through. I know that feeling of displacement will pass. Each day gets a little clearer. This whole experience has been just a page in our book and the ending is not yet written!

Thank you Erin for laying a foundation of information. There are places to get assistance that can be found in the **Resources and Support** section of this book, so don't hesitate to call on those who can help. After hearing from Erin, you can also use this information to know how to help any other family going through this. It's always great to be able to step up and offer much needed care.

"God gave us hugs for times when there are no words."

– Rick Anderson

Loss and Grief

Most likely there will come a time in your years of military service when you'll know someone or the family of someone who's loved one didn't return on the same plane as everyone else. Times of conflict bring times of loss and grief. It's unfair to write a book dealing with reunion and reintegration without bringing to light how to be of service in the tough times.

I met an amazing family who has dealt with this greatest of losses and chose to share their journey with you. They opened their home and hearts to me, and we spent many hours getting to know each other. Their experience is the most real way I have of talking about this in a manner that will help.

Many articles and books have been written about losses that have taken place. As you'll hear later, Christopher's story has been written about in the book *Final Salute* by Jim Sheeler. But of all that has been written about Christopher and others like him, this is the first time that the Anderson family shared it in their words, rather than another person writing about this most sensitive yet necessary area on their behalf. These are their words. Other than some editing for clarity, I have not changed what they've shared. They have written from the heart, and I've tried to honor their words and feelings.

As you're reading this chapter, I don't know where you might be in this scenario (parent, spouse, friend, comrade, etc.) but sharing one family's story may just help you find your place. If it doesn't apply to you at this time then I am grateful; but if it does, then the messages of comfort, help and hope that you'll experience in these pages may help you find your peace.

The Road Home for Christopher
by Rick and Debbie Anderson

On December 4, 2006, HM3 (FMF) Christopher "Doc" Anderson, a Navy corpsman was killed in action in Ramadi Iraq. He was assigned to the 1st Battalion, 6th Marines, Alpha Company. His squad call themselves the "Misfits." My name is Rick, my wife's name is Debbie, and our son's name is Kyle. We are Christopher's father, mother and brother. I retired from the United States Navy after 20 years of service, and six of those years were as a Navy SEAL. Debbie's father served 26 years in the Navy as well. We both understand how the Navy and the military work, but neither of us had ever been trained in how to handle the loss of our son Christopher.

God smiled on us and comforted us in a time of great pain, and for that we were indeed blessed. We would like to share Christopher's Road Home so that you can better understand what happens to the family when someone in the military is killed in action. Our hope is that by sharing what happened to us, the decisions we made, and the many ways we were blessed by those who stepped forward to help, you might be able to help someone else who is forced to deal with the loss of a loved one.

There are three things we would like to share about Christopher's coming home:

1. **The Process** – starting with notification of his death through his burial at Arlington National Cemetery and the changes in our lives.

2. **The Choices** we made that helped us deal with losing Christopher, and

3. **The Deeds** – some of the wonderful things that family, old friends and new friends did to help this difficult time go a bit smoother.

The Process

We planned to go to North Carolina in May 2007 to meet our sailor when he got off the bus. We looked forward to meeting the Marines and other corpsman he served with in Iraq and hearing all the stories about his deployment and the things that he and "His Marines," as Christopher called them, had accomplished. Instead, on an unusually warm December night, we got the "Knock on the Door."

Knock on the Door

The Navy Notification team consisted of a Chaplain, a Chief Petty Officer who was the Casualty Assistance Calls Officer (CACO), and a First Class Petty Officer.

Much of it would be just as you might expect, our disbelief, the casualty affairs officer bravely and professionally reading the official message, while somehow managing not to succumb to the overwhelming emotion in the room. Everyone was trying to comfort each other. The chaplain, cautiously and tactfully tried to discover what we believed in so he knew how to best offer support. The corpsman, trying to blend in, watched out for any signs of possible physical distress on our part. Four things happened that night that had a major impact on our lives.

1. Sometime during this first night, as I realized there was nothing I could do to bring Christopher back or stop this from happening, I decided it was time for God and me to have a conversation. I asked, "God, what do you want me to do with this? I don't like this now, and I'm going to like it even less later. God, what do you want me to do with this?" I know that putting what I could not handle into God's hands was the absolute best thing I could do then, and I am even more convinced of that now.

2. Debbie and I were talking with the chaplain and Debbie asked him, "How do I deal with this?" His response was simple and profound and was one of the guides we used to get us through the process, and we still use today. He said, "You will set the example for people to follow." Debbie took that statement as a responsibility to represent and protect Christopher, our Navy and our troops in a very positive and respectful way.

I took it to mean that during this stressful time as people approached us, ever so cautiously, that they would be looking to us for some indication as to how they should interact with us. I felt it was up to us to demonstrate some form of positive leadership so as we and everyone who came in contact with us were tossed around in the powerful storm of emotions, we could maintain and encourage the most positive attitude possible.

3. Then Debbie said something that surprised me. She said, "You know people will need to come to our home." She said it in a way that made it clear to me that we were going to need to share this time in our lives with others, and we need to welcome them into our home. Inviting a large group of people into our home is not something we normally do, so to hear this come out of my wife's mouth, with such peace and confidence, was truly amazing. And then the highly organized and in control woman I married simply "shut down" and stayed that way for nearly a month. She was still talking, crying and sharing, but organization and control took a vacation. I saw this as Kyle's and my opportunity to take care of her.

At this point, we chose to share Christopher with anyone who felt the need to share with us. Not everyone in our situation does this. Some choose to keep things very private. Each family must choose what is right for them.

4. As things progressed, important and challenging decisions were thrust upon us. We asked ourselves this simple question before we made any decisions: "If we do this, what good thing will come from it?" This question was asked with the intention of helping someone other than ourselves. We still ask this question regularly.

Meeting the Plane

We met Christopher at Denver International Airport. It was dark, but it wasn't warm anymore. We continued to cry, as the military in their dress uniforms, respectfully and with great dignity, unloaded the casket.

There were many people who helped us that night. For the most part, they were people who did what they knew how to do. We arrived at the airport early so the airport fire department welcomed us into their building and offered us hot drinks, allowing us to get out of the car and escape some of the tension as we waited. On our way out of the airport we saw the fire department in their dress uniforms standing in the flashing lights of their equipment saluting as we went by. It helped. Christopher had friends in the police department who graciously arranged a police escort. It helped. The Patriot Guard (*a group of volunteer motorcycle riders who provide escorts and will shield families from protesters, if necessary) were there to escort us back to Longmont. It helped. On the way out of the airport we stopped and said thank you to those who came out to escort us. We found it was important to not only notice the blessings, but also to acknowledge them. This continued as we brought Christopher to the funeral home. People were standing along the street. They were waiting at the funeral home. Some held candles, some held flags, some had signs, and each one was a gift to us. People were doing what they could and it helped. It still does every time we think of it, which is often.

Help at Home

Our world was turned upside down, we needed help, and God provided it. My wife's sister Sherry flew into town immediately and helped provide organization and supervision for the many things going on. Two of our friends spent nearly a week taking turns screening phone calls, answering the door, organizing food that was being dropped by, keeping the place clean, and tending to the various needs of those visiting with us. Another man assisted us with the overall organization of things, and he brought in a friend who had experience working with the media. When he first walked into our house the phone was ringing every fifteen minutes. He stayed with us for nearly a week, took control of the media frenzy and helped us work with the TV, radio and newspaper reporters. When he walked in we didn't even know his name! Now two years later, he's the type of friend that you hug when you meet. A police officer made arrangements for extra security patrols in our neighborhood. The neighbor children attached flags to all the lampposts on our section of the street. There was food everywhere! People just stepped forward as needed. Some organized the chaos, some made sure there was toilet paper in the bathroom. Others simply sat with us when we needed company. They were all blessings, and we don't know what we would've done without them.

One afternoon, a brave woman, with tears in her eyes knocked on our door. She was carrying a small plant that looked like a miniature Christmas tree. She has two sons in the Navy and said that she simply needed to meet us, tell us how she felt, and offer her help. She worked at a local hotel, and made arrangements for a special rate for all the family that was coming in from out of town. Her job at the hotel was to prepare the morning continental breakfast and help the hotel guests feel welcome. She went the extra mile and did exactly that for our family and friends.

Dealing with the Media

We chose to talk to the media and share Christopher's story. Here are three things we learned that we found helpful.

The first place the media will look for information is online. They will go to MySpace, Facebook, or any other online networking site. Whatever they find may very well be published in the newspaper or shown on the TV news. Tip: Be aware of all the personal information that is exposed on those sites. You shouldn't post anything that you don't want everyone to have access to.

Delegate someone to handle the media for you and look at who you'll talk to and who you won't. You can be picky about who you give information to. You don't have to talk to anyone you don't want to. You are in charge, not the media.

You can tell the media that you will be releasing a statement at some specific time in the future. That will relieve some of the immediate pressure.

The Funeral

The receiving line wasn't planned; it just seemed to happen by itself. In addition to friends and family, there were many veterans from various wars who attended. Many looked like they were in more pain than we were. You could see it in their eyes as they talked with us. I suspect they reflected on their own losses and how they were treated when they returned.

The Patriot Guard provided an escort and lined the street with flags. People volunteered to help set up the church for the funeral while others made food for the reception. Someone brought white doves and released them at the service. Another caring person took a whole series of pictures and a couple weeks later left them on our front porch, anonymously. A man rode his horse and carried a big American flag, and posted himself next to the turnoff to the church. Two years later, he sent us a photo of him on his horse outside the church, framed it, and attached a wonderful letter that makes us feel good every time we read it.

Arlington

Christopher had specifically requested to be buried in Arlington National Cemetery if he was killed in action. Once again the Patriot Guard was there as were family members of Christopher's squad mates in Iraq, and other sailors he had served with, many who we had never met.

There are still occasions, even after two years, when we will reflect back to that time. The finality of it all makes us sad, but then we think of those who went out of their way to be there that day. We can't help but be impressed with their caring and kindness. These reflections continue to help us every time we think about Arlington.

Christopher's Belongings

About five weeks after Christopher was killed, the belongings he had with him in Iraq were delivered to our home by the CACO. The Marines had gone through, cleaned, folded and organized everything neatly. One of the most wonderful things that we found were personally written letters from his squad mates comforting us and telling us how they felt about Christopher. They are something we will treasure the rest of our lives along with every gift and card that has been sent to us.

We have a room set up with many of Christopher's favorite things and his awards. It is healing and it gives us an opportunity to share some of our memories with friends, family and any other interested people. If someone is visiting and shows an interest in this chapter of our life, we always offer to show them.

Meeting the "Misfits"

May 2007 came. It was the month Christopher was supposed to come home. We were still on our way to camp Lejeune, but instead of meeting his bus, we were there to attend a memorial service.

Christopher was one of eleven lost on that deployment, and each of the fallen were represented with traditional rifle, helmet, dog tags and boots, as well as a beautiful portrait done in pencil, donated by an artist. In addition to the ceremony that applied to us all, a comrade of each of the fallen told a personal story about their friend. It was truly a blessing to be able to attend, and Debbie, Kyle and I each had our own personal reasons for wanting to be there. Debbie needed to know that when he was killed that he was surrounded by people who loved and cared about him. Kyle and I wanted to meet the men who served with Christopher. We needed to know what kind of men they were and we needed to know that the official story of Christopher's death we had received was true.

Something else became very obvious to us. These guys were hurting just as bad, or maybe even worse, than we were. They hadn't had the same support and opportunity to grieve that we had. The very day after Christopher's death they were back on patrol in enemy territory without their brother "Doc." We saw this as a chance to help them work through the loss of a comrade. We understand that their instinctive responsibility is to protect. As one of the Marines explained to us, just prior to Christopher's deployment, "It's our job to get between the bullets and Doc. We don't know how to take the bullets out of Doc, but Doc can take them out of us."

At that time, they were comforting words to us, but that time had passed. We knew that Christopher was in a better place, and I knew that neither God, Christopher nor we wanted these good men to carry around a burden that wasn't theirs to carry. I shared with them what I told Christopher before he deployed: "When you do the best you can with what you have, in the time God gives you to do it, that's all anyone can do or ask of you. The rest is in God's hands, not yours! Sometimes God's plan and our plans don't match. You do your part and let God do His." Then I told them, "We are proud of you and everything you did for Christopher."

Something special happened later that evening. Christopher's squad took time away from their families to have dinner with us. We will always remember the stories they told about Christopher, but what made me the happiest was to see them talk about Christopher and laugh. The squad treated us like family and we them. We cried, laughed, had a drink or two and shared a meal. This is exactly what Christopher would have wanted.

Some of the Misfits still call us occasionally, and it always makes our day to talk with them and see how they are doing. We may only talk a few minutes, but the good feelings from that phone call last and last.

Your "New Normal," and Where to Go From Here

I believe that if you have a better understanding of what may be going on with a family who has suffered a loss, you'll be better prepared to help and support them.

Everything in our world changed after Christopher was killed, and it will never be the same again. We are slowly developing a new normal, and are still not sure what it is or what it should be.

One of the biggest changes is our relationship with Christopher even though he's no longer with us physically. He is still with us in our minds and hearts, and the minds and hearts of many other people as well.

We also know that Christopher is with God. We believe that when we make our commitment to let God be in charge of our lives, that we are in Him and He is in us. It's comforting to know that Christopher is not very far away, and that one day we will be together again.

We still talk about Christopher regularly, especially when it comes to what we call "Christopher Things." Those are things that happen throughout our day and in our lives that wouldn't ever have happened if it hadn't been for Christopher; like having the opportunity to contribute to this book or talking to one of the many new friends we've made because of Christopher. Christopher not only changed our lives but also the lives of many others. We like to talk about and celebrate these changes and the opportunities that come with them.

We know that Christopher wouldn't want us to be upset and crying all the time, but crying can be a good thing! It's one of God's gifts to us. Emotions and feelings need to come out that can't always be expressed through words. Crying provides us that much-needed outlet. Sometimes people are hesitant to talk with us, particularly about Christopher, for fear that they may upset us and make us cry. That's not the way it works! Dealing with our loss is a natural part of our life. Like Debbie says, "It's not your fault I'm crying. It is a gift you give that I feel safe enough with you to express this emotion." Toughing it out is the wrong thing to do. Your emotional energy will come out whether you want it to or not, so the choice you have is **how** it's going to come out. If you pick a healthy release like crying, things will get better . . . at least for a while. If you hold it in, it has the potential to take your health, mentally and physically. **Cry now or pay later.**

We have our good days and we have our bad days and it's important to take a break and rest when you need to. Don't answer the door or phone while you take time to "regroup."

We know that some times of the year will be more challenging than others, like Christopher's birthday, the month of December (Christopher was killed December 4, and we were not able to bury him until the 27th), and Memorial Day. Those are the times when notes, letters and phone calls from our friends and family are especially helpful. We do our best during those times to stay busy with constructive, positive things because for us it's all part of our new normal.

The Choices

Positive Attitude

The choices we make every day have a huge impact on our lives and that seems to be amplified when you unexpectedly lose someone close to you. Usually the unhealthy choices are the easiest ones to make, so find ways to turn these around.

Here's an example of what I mean: At first, Debbie wanted 24 white roses—one for each year of Christopher's life—and one red one for each year that has passed since his death. It seemed like a good idea at the time. Then we realized that **loss** was not what we should focus on. We needed to celebrate what we had, which was being blessed by 24 years of Christopher in our lives. So now we celebrate Christopher's life with only the 24 roses every December 4th. Framing life's events in a positive way makes a huge difference.

Getting over "The Ugly"

Sometimes, as we walk on the path of our new life, we see what appears to be a huge ugly roadblock right in front of us. It's very easy to perceive this obstacle as a major challenge even when it's not.

The truth is, once we go over, through or around the ugly bump on the path, we find that when we get past it, it wasn't as ugly as it looked, or as hard as we thought. We find that we are a little bit stronger, a little more confident, and a little more prepared for the next ugly bump. Most of the time, we just need a little encouragement to move forward. The more we do it, the better we get at it. We are fortunate because Debbie, Kyle and I have each other and we can go through this together. Not everybody does, so a little encouragement from you can go a long way.

Advice from Debbie

I love to talk about Christopher, so when someone asks me my son's name or branch of service I feel they are opening a window of opportunity for me to share about

Christopher. There are times when I don't feel up to saying more than just answering the questions, but if the person shows to be a good listener I might want to share a lot more. Being able to talk about how, where and when Christopher died is a way for me to deal with this tragic reality. I find it so amazing that we have had death since the beginning of time, but we (including myself) still do not know how to talk about it. We all say, "I don't know what to say," or "I'm so sorry." I have learned there are no perfect words, so I decided to not get caught up in the words but to pay attention to the heart. Any time someone starts a conversation with words or with just a look, I feel comforted to know they care.

170 Rick and I found it to be a huge help to meet other Gold Star families. We discovered how comforting it is to talk with others going through the same thing. They are so much easier to talk with because it's like you're saying to each other, "You're not going to shock me with your story and I won't shock you with mine. We're on the same page and the same place." We want people to know that we LIKE to talk about Christopher. They shouldn't be afraid to be a part of the conversation.

171 **Thank you cards:** For me, I wanted to let people know their cards or gifts were received and appreciated. My neighbors and friends wanted to help me with something, so we had an "envelope addressing, stuffing and stamping" get together. It was great for me to let my friends read some of the wonderful and kind words people wrote from all over the country. It was truly helpful because the task of doing this alone was too great, and I really wanted to let everyone know how truly grateful we are that they thought of us.

172 Finally, please be patient and understanding. We don't always respond to, and receive things, in the manner they were given. Sometimes we just couldn't answer the door or the phone. You are important to us, but our emotions have taken over and we just can't respond to you at that exact moment. Please forgive us and do not take it personally. We would love to have another opportunity to visit with you.

The Deeds

Other Things People Did that Meant a Lot to Us

(**Author's note:** As you read the ideas below, I want you to visualize it from a different perspective. For example, if a school class did something special for the Andersons and you're a teacher, think about something your class could do to help a family.)

It is important to us to keep Christopher's memory alive and well. We were especially in need of good Christopher memories right after he was killed. What brought us the most comfort came from people sharing those memories. We loved hearing about things he did that helped make someone's life better. Even the smallest memories were welcomed. For example:

- A high school friend brought over her year book to share what Christopher wrote to her.

- Friends brought over pictures of Christopher and shared the stories about those days—everything from Christopher giving them advice that was helpful, to finding out that he took the time to listen to someone so they had a chance to feel better.

173 Don't be afraid to contact a family if you feel you should. We received anonymous letters, letters that didn't spell the name correctly or name his exact branch of service. They were all welcomed and appreciated. The bottom line is it makes us feel good to know that people care and try to understand. Knowing that the American people support our troops and understand the sacrifice they are making to keep our country safe gives us great comfort.

174 All cards are welcomed. In the card you send, include your email address and phone number. So often people feel they need to get those cards or letters out to families immediately, but I found that going to the mail box six months or a year later and finding a card from someone who wanted to let us know they remember Christopher and are thinking of us made us feel wonderful. I believe it can never be too late or too many years after Christopher's death to hear from someone who remembers him.

175 In the middle school where Christopher attended, the library is surrounded by glass walls. Painted on these glass walls are famous Americans and events in U.S. history. Someone made arrangements for a local artist to put a picture of Christopher in his dress uniform on this wall in front of an American flag. This is very special not only to us but to the neighborhood children who consider Christopher their friend and "big brother." We visit that picture at least once a year.

176 Someone contacted a local politician and requested one of the flags that had flown over the capitol. The flag was delivered to us with a letter and the date the flag flew over the capitol in Christopher's honor.

Rick shared, "One day shortly after Christopher was killed I saw three familiar looking young men loitering by our mailbox. As it turned out they were involved in the Navy delayed entry program at the same time Christopher had been. They felt they needed to do something, so they decided to come over and watch the house for us. From that humble beginning a friendship has grown, and we enjoy talking with them periodically to see what is going on in their lives.

Things People Did to Include Christopher's Memory in Their Lives:

Christopher was supposed to be a groomsman at our niece Tiffany's wedding. Since Christopher couldn't be there, Tiffany had a small teddy bear in a Navy uniform made, and the bear attended as one of the groomsmen. The Navy bear also did quite a bit of dancing at the reception with some beautiful young women. When we see the Navy Bear in the wedding photos it makes us smile.

One of the squad members who served with Christopher lit a memorial candle in his honor as part of his wedding ceremony. They also listed Christopher in their wedding bulletin and sent us a copy, as well as photographs of the wedding.

Several of the Misfits have Doc Anderson memorial tattoos. Not being a tattoo person, I actually tried to talk them out of it, but I can't help thinking of the tattoos, and the men who have them. With a smile on my face I wonder that if someday, when someone sees grandpa with his shirt off, will a little voice ask, "Who's Doc Anderson, and why is his name on you?"

An elementary school class in Loveland, Colorado sent Valentine's Day cards to us that first year.

Over a year after Christopher was killed a little boy wrote us a note and delivered it in person on Veterans Day.

The following story tells of a gift from one of Christopher's squad mates, Johnathan. Not only is this a wonderful memory for us, but Johnathan says that it helped him see that life goes on. The San Diego Padres were Christopher's favorite baseball team, and while they were deployed Johnathan and Christopher made plans to attend a game together. After Christopher died, I received this email from Johnathan: *I wanted to let you know that on the 3rd I was able to get tickets to a Washington Nationals game. I don't care much for the Nats, but they're who San Diego was playing. I knew I needed to see that game. I bought four tickets. I went, and so did my father and brother. I used the fourth ticket for Christopher. I had the gentleman at the gate scan Christopher's ticket so that he would be on the attendance roster. I know he was there with me, and I know that it's wasn't about baseball and it never will be about baseball again. It will be about Christopher and me. That was our game. I took a yellow ribbon and two American flags with me and set them on Christopher's seat. I took some pictures and included them with this email. I have the ticket and I would like to send it to you. By the way, the Padres won 7-3. It was Christopher's day at the park.*

One of the biggest blessings God provided us came in one of the last ways I would have ever expected. A Pulitzer prize-winning newspaper journalist wrote an incredible book. If you would truly like to understand the journey taken by the families of those who've been killed in action, you should read *Final Salute* by Jim Sheeler. Jim didn't just write about five men who were killed in action and their families. He shared this part of our lives with us and allowed us to share it with you in a very clear and intimate way. The understanding you get by reading this book will change your life, in a good direction. You will get a chance to see the love, respect and honor freely and generously poured out by the American people in tribute to their fallen military. Anyone who leads men into battle, any politician who has influence over our military, or for that matter anyone with a vote, should read this book.

I would also like to thank the veterans, especially those from the Vietnam era. I'm not sure the spectacular change from protest to support in the American attitude would've happened without their dedication, hard work and involvement. God bless you all. Rick, Debbie and Kyle Anderson may be reached through: Rick@DocAndersonFamily.com.

"They told their story with such grace. It makes me thankful to be an American." These were the first words I heard from someone who read this sensitive account of a most challenging time. Grace . . . I couldn't have selected a better word because the story takes you to places you pray you never have to go, yet it leaves you with a message of hope, understanding and strength. I'm so glad I got a chance to know the Andersons, and I'm honored to call them friends.

Chapter 4
Living a Prepared Life

Living a Prepared Life

◆ ◆ ◆

Redeployment realities . . .

1.5 million American troops have been deployed
One-third served at least two tours in a combat zone
70,000 have been deployed three times
20,000 have been deployed at least five times[7]

I realize that it seems weird to talk about redeploying when you're just now planning your return home, but one soldier said, "Since we've had some experiences with back-to-back deployments, we had added another phase that we call 'pre-redeployment prep.' It occurs after reunion and reintegration but before the next deployment. We try to get a jump start on all the deployment tasks prior to the next time so that when official word comes about the deployment, we have more time to spend with one another and our family. Things like updating our wills and power of attorney, reviewing insurance policies, and scheduling home repairs can be done at our leisure without the pressure of nearing the deployment timeline. We know there will be another deployment, so why not do the preparation on our own schedule instead of one that is forced on us and takes away our time?" Good thing to think about.

177 Do a home improvement project together. Evaluate a few things that need to be done and see if you have the skills and talents to do them together. Believe it or not, my husband and I found that we work well together when we are wallpapering or painting a room. I know, most couples think we're crazy and they say they could never do that! My husband is mathematical and logical, and I have the creative side, so I conceded to how he wanted to measure and use small brushes to cut around trims, and he conceded to my suggestions of what would look best. We also found that Larry likes the measuring/cutting part of wallpapering, and I like getting up on the ladder and hanging it. When we paint, I'm the one who takes the masking tape/paper and covers all the areas not to be painted, and he comes after me and cuts and rolls. Voila, a newly painted interior and three wallpapered rooms with very little arguing. Try it, you'll like it.

178 From Victoria: "While my husband has been deployed, I have been keeping a 'Deployment Notebook.' In this book I keep notes of stuff that is going on at home. For example, there has been some substantial construction done on our house. I have been making notes of what was done, dates, who did the work, and cost. Same goes for auto repairs. Also, it's a good place to note contact information of people who have offered their assistance in various areas. Of course, I share this with him in emails and IM's, but it seems to be helpful to have it all gathered in one location. When my husband gets home, he can peruse the notebook and read about all the details of the past year here so it won't be so foreign to him. It helps me, too, in that when I reread what I have accomplished, I feel empowered!"

As we were talking, I often heard that deployment orders came so quickly that it left very little time to prepare some deployment remembrances for the kids before it was time to leave. I share this because it was one of the things that a deployed person regretted most. They'd say, "I wish I had known or done that before I left." Now that you've been through it and we're talking about the possibility of redeployments down the line, you can remedy that this time. Below are a few of the ideas from the second book, *I'm Already Home . . . Again* that were most popular. These are best done before you leave. Just remember to leave time in your schedule.

First, I've been talking about Flat Daddy® as one of the most used ideas for families with children for over six years now. Earlier in the book you might recall I talked about how families ceremoniously gave Flat Daddy® a well deserved rest by relegating him to the closet. Just in case you didn't know what I was talking about, please read on and consider one for your children.

179 Cindy and her eight-year-old daughter, Sarah, introduce you to Flat Daddy®. Three months after Dave was deployed, Cindy took a "waist up" photo of him (dressed in fatigues) to a local print shop. They enlarged it to life size and mounted it on foam board—like a big, two-dimensional paper doll. "He was missing so many family gatherings," said Cindy. Flat Daddy® then traveled to graduations, weddings, and other celebrations where he took his rightful place in the photographs. Copies were sent to Dave overseas so he could see where he'd been while he was gone! Cindy keeps an album at home of everywhere Flat Daddy® has been . . . even tucking Sarah into bed. This was the real reason that Flat Daddy® was created—to give Sarah a daily visual reminder of Dave so that she'd recognize him when he returned from Iraq after fifteen months. Sarah had just turned one year old when he left. Speaking of Sarah, when he was deployed, the real Dave received a Flat Sarah, minus the foam board, so he could see how much she'd grown.

Those of you who have heard me present at your family readiness conference know how this idea has taken off! In many families, Flat Daddy® has held watch over Halloween candy and visited Chuck E. Cheese™.

Special ideas that involve photos where the deploying servicemember is in them of course should be scheduled ahead of time. The key here is not to make it too big of a deal. I think that when families think they have to get all cleaned up and trudge down to the photo studio for a posed picture, they put it off. I know I do. It's just too much work! I like this next idea because it served more than one purpose. It got all the families in the unit involved in a more informal setting and also let the family have something useful that they could use to let others communicate with their loved one while deployed. You can either arrange it for the unit as a whole or just do it for yourself and have a neighbor come in to take the photo.

180 A unit had pictures taken of each soldier with their kids, spouse or significant other at the armory. The soldier was dressed in uniform against an all black background. These photos were beautiful and a bit more formal than a snapshot. Embossed on it is the soldier's name, email address, and *Thank You for Your Prayers*. Some families had wallet-size copies made to give out to those who would like to send a note. It's so much better than jotting the information on a scrap of paper every time someone asks for it.

Children who are about nine years old and above can now think logically about what's happening. If you've been through deployments before, you know how keeping those thoughts hidden can hurt. Before you head out again, sit down together and do what the family below did. The person who offered this suggestion said that it truly did help.

181 Have the child make a list (as specific as possible) of all the things they are worried about regarding the deployment. It's a good idea to have the parent sitting with them, but they shouldn't contribute to or edit any of what's being listed. Next, have the child take list #1 and divide it into two separate lists: the first is a list of things they can do something about, along with ideas of steps they can take. This is where a parent can help, but only to act as a sounding board or to help generate the action steps. The second list contains the things you have no control over and can do nothing about. Then encourage the child to allow himself/herself to let go of what's on this second list and only focus on those things they can control. That should take some of the burden off.

Finally, remember to do anything ahead of time that requires your voice and/or image. Things like making a video/DVD of you reading a child's favorite bedtime stories or recording your voice for them to play throughout the day. Maybe you can record a few special messages to be played on dates you might be missing such as a birthday, graduation, Christmas or Hanukah, etc. One woman wrote that she took her kids to Build-A-Bear® Workshop and they each made a bear in an Army uniform. They have uniforms for all branches. She put a small squeezable voice recorder box (they have those there) inside the bear's paw. Her husband recorded a short personal message to each child on their bear's recorder before he left. Every time one of the children wanted to feel close to Dad, all it took was a hug of the bear and a squeeze of it's paw to hear Dad's voice. As you can see this works for kids of any age—and also spouses! (Leave a little part of yourself all over the house.)

◆

As we come to a close and move forward with the life God has given us to live, remember that there are always those around who care. Sometimes you just have to know where to look for them. Above all, as you settle back into the life you knew before you left, remember these two pieces of advice:

Go slowly.

Put trust in those around you.

Epilogue

◆ ◆ ◆

It's been so difficult to know when to stop writing! So many great ideas and good resources keep coming across my desk that I keep thinking just have to be included. I told you at the beginning of the book that that would happen. But if I don't stop, I'll never get the information I already have into your hands. So I'll say, now that my third book to you is completed, I feel that we've become good friends. Over these past six+ years I've talked with so many of you through email or over the phone. I have friends all over this great country whom I've never met, but wish I could. I also wish that every civilian could shake hands with you and come to know you the way I have. You are amazing people, and I'm proud of each servicemember and the families we hope to keep strong. Saying Thank You just doesn't seem like enough sometimes, and I trust that you know that we're looking out for you every day, even when you don't know it.

I'm closing this book in a way that has become a tradition for me in all my books—with one of the most wonderful emails I have ever received. I believe that it sums up most of what we've been talking about all along. It touched me so much that I have it hanging on the wall in my office. It was a reply to me from my son who was 600 miles away at college, following an email I sent to him advising him of a safety alert for college campuses. It shows that the love and care you give each other is always appreciated, so never stop working on it. Here's what he sent back:

Hey Mom, I just wanted to say thank you for that little bit of advice. I will also make sure to tell some of the other people around here. I had no idea that this was a problem. I would have definitely been one to pull over right away for a car with sirens. Thanks for always looking out for me. I know I may get embarrassed sometimes or even upset because you do it so much, but don't listen to me or ever pay attention to that. You always seem to find some way to help me out and I am grateful. You always know what to do. Thanks for looking out for me and loving me as much as you do. Have a wonderful day and I love you. Tell Dad the same for me, please. Talk to you soon.

Bryan

I love you, too, Bryan. Goodnight.

Resources and Support

"Resilient military families don't want to be rescued, they want resources so they can help themselves."

– Gen Craig R. McKinley

Resources and Support

I found many good resources to help with challenges like Post Traumatic Stress Disorder (PTSD), reunion advice for families and communities, deployment cycle support, and transition for active duty service to civilian life. Rather than provide synopses of these programs, I've listed many of them in this **Resources and Support** section of the book. One booklet that I really did like is called

———————◆———————

Reintegration: Beyond Reunion –
A guide for service members and their families.
Ask your support office if they have a copy for you. If not, you can order them by calling toll free 1-800-628-7733, or visiting *www.channing-bete.com* and asking for item number PS92753.

———————◆———————

Education

GI Bill
www.gibill/va/gov
Information regarding the Montgomery GI Bill.

National Veterans Upward Bound
http://www.navub.org/
VUB staff and instructors assist veterans by developing, improving, and extending educational access and opportunities to eligible veterans through academic needs assessment, instruction, enrichment, and other academic support activities.

Scholarships for Military Children
www.militaryscholar.org
This program was created in recognition of the contributions of military families to the readiness of the fighting force and to celebrate the role of the commissary in the military family community. It is the intent of the program that a scholarship funded through contributions be awarded annually for each commissary operated by the Defense Commissary Agency worldwide.

University of Phoenix
www.uopxmilitary.com
Degree programs designed specifically for military personnel and special military tuition rates are offered with specific coursework and programs designed to fit the demands of a military lifestyle.

Veterans Fund
www.veteransfund.org/index.html
Apply for scholarships or make a donation to help send a vet to school.

Employment

All Retail Jobs
www.allretailjobs.com
Is the largest career and recruiting board designed for retail employers. All Retail Jobs serves to place employees in careers from retail executives, store management, buyers, merchandisers, sales and even part-time associates.

CPOL: Employment Index
www.acpol.army.mil/employment
A comprehensive database of civilian employment opportunities with the military.

Career Command Post
www.careercommandpost.com
A job resource and information Center.

Department of Labor
www.dol.gov/dol/audience/aud-veterans.htm
A shortcut to information and services the Department of Labor (DOL) offers veterans.

Helmets to Hardhats
www.helmetstohardhats.org
This is the fastest way for Military, Reservists & Guardsmen to transition from active duty to a career in the construction industry.

Hire Veterans
www.hireveterans.com
They locate relevant jobs for veterans offered by world class companies in the U.S. and abroad. Also provides employers access to resumes and job postings so that they can reach veteran job seekers.

Hire Vets First
www.hirevetsfirst.gov
Provides resources to match employment opportunities with veterans.

Job Accommodation Network
www.jan.wvu.edu
One of several Office of Disability Employment Policy (ODEP) projects with a mission to facilitate the employment and retention of workers with disabilities by providing employers, employment providers, people with disabilities, their family members and other interested parties with information on job accommodations, entrepreneurship, and related subjects.

Jobs 4 HR
www.jobs4hr.com
Offers a jobseeker numerous tools to manage their career: A job database, career email notification, resume database and distribution services, calendar of career events, continuing education guides.

Jobs in Logistics
www.jobsinlogistics.com
The first and largest career and recruiting board specializing in Logistics, Manufacturing, Supply Chain, Transportation, Purchasing, Freight Forwarding, Distribution, Warehousing, 3PL and Materials Management.

Career Center for Combat Wounded and Disabled Veterans
www.military.com/hero/0,,WVC_AlwaysASoldier,00.html
Information about Army Material Command's "Always A Soldier Program" that provides continuing support to Warfighters beyond their active duty service.

Military Spouse Career Center
www.military.com/spouse1
The Center's web site was developed and is operated by Monster and Military.com under contract on behalf of the Department of Defense. Serving America, Military Spouse Career Center supports spouses and families by providing access to career opportunities, training information and education options.

Military Exits
www.militaryexits.com
Job placement assistance for all discharging service members, spouses and dependents.

Military Job Zone
www.militaryjobzone.com
Specializing in military recruiting and placement, veteran job placement, and other transition services. MJZ works with transitioning military members and veterans to find civilian careers

Military Stars
www.militarystars.com
The nation's largest military career expo company and placement firm.

Quintessential Careers
www.quintcareers.com
Offers more than 3,500 pages of free college, career, and job-search content to empower and drive success in life.

Spouses to Teachers
www.spousestoteachers.com
"Spouses to Teachers" is a DOD project designed to assist spouses of active duty and reserve military members to become public school teachers.

Transition Assistance Online
www.taonline.com
The largest single source of transition assistance information and tools for todays separating military. On this web site service members (both prior and current) can find the resources needed to transition from military service to the perfect civilian career.

USA Jobs
www.usajobs.opm.gov
Official Federal government job site that serves as a one stop source for all federal jobs and employment information.

US Navy Civilian Hiring and Recruitment
www.chart.donhr.navy.mil
Department of the Navy's civilian hiring and recruitment site.

Vet Jobs
www.vetjobs.com
Assists ALL members of "The United States Military Family" including Officer and Enlisted, Active Duty, Transitioning Military, Reservists, Veterans, Retirees, of the Air Force, Army, Coast Guard, Marine Corps, Merchant Marine, National Guard, Navy, NOAA and Public Health Service along with Trailing Spouses, Eligible Former Spouses, Widows, Widowers and Dependents and DOD civilians.

GI JOBS
www.gijobs.net/content/top50.cfm
Military friendly employers rated based on benefit packages, number of veteran employees and flexibility with guard and reserve schedules.

Financial Assistance

ACORN Housing
www.acornhousing.org
As a national non-profit they provide free housing counseling to low and moderate income homebuyers including one-on-one mortgage loan counseling, first-time homebuyer classes, and help obtaining affordable mortgages through unique lending partnerships.

Children of Fallen Soldiers Relief Fund
www.cfsrf.org
Provides College Grants and Financial Assistance to surviving children and spouses of our U.S. military service members who have lost their lives in the Iraq and Afghanistan wars. Assists disabled service member families as well.

College Scholarships
http://www.collegescholarships.org/scholarships/family.htm
Links to state specific, branch specific scholarships that are available to service members and their families.

Home Loan
www.homeloans.va.gov
Answers and resources for VA home loans

Home for Our Troops
www.homesforourtroops.org
Assists severely injured servicemen and women and their immediate families by accepting donations of money, building materials and professional labor while coordinating the process of building a new home or adapting an existing home for handicapped accessibility.

Money Management International
www.moneymanagement.org
Provides professional financial guidance, credit counseling, community-wide educational programs, debt management assistance and housing counseling to consumers via phone, Internet and in-person sessions.

Operation Family Fund
www.operationfamilyfund.org
Provides financial grants to injured servicemembers and families of the those who have been injured or killed as a part of the Global War on Terrorism. Focuses on a goal of financial self-sufficiency.

Our Fallen Soldier
www.ourfallensoldier.com
Offers free web pages for fallen heroes to be remembered. Also provides financial support for loved ones, sponsors camps for children and spouses of the fallen as well as rehabilitation programs.

Operation Hero Miles
www.heromiles.org
Travelers donate unused frequent flyer miles to the Pentagon so troops and families can use them to get free tickets. This program also gives family members of wounded servicemen and women free plane tickets to visit their loved ones recovering at military hospitals across the country.

Pentagon Federal Credit Union Foundation
www.pentagonfoundation.org
This nonprofit national charity works to meet unmet needs of military personnel and their families in the areas of financial literacy, housing and support for the wounded.

Project We Remember
www.projectweremember.org
Dedicated to raising funds for individuals and non-profit organizations that provide support to our military families in need.

USA Cares
www.usacares.us
Provides military families with financial and advocacy support in their time of need.

Giving Back

Commissaries
http://www.commissaries.com/certificheck/index.cfm
The "Gift of Groceries" program helps meet the needs of Guard and Reserve families. You can purchase a certificate for someone you know or donate to a needy service family through this website.

A Million Thanks
www.amillionthanks.org
A year-round campaign to show U.S. Military Men and Women, past and present, our appreciation for their sacrifices, dedication, and service to our country through letters, emails, cards, prayers, and thoughts.

Any Soldier
anysoldier.com
Provides information and assistance for sending support to a soldier in harm's way. Includes addresses to send packages as well as how to send items and what to send.

Defenders of Freedom
www.defendersoffreedom.us
A 501 (c) 3 non profit organization with the purpose of raising money to support our troops who are currently deployed around the world.

Freedom Alliance
www.freedomalliance.org
Their mission is to advance the American heritage of freedom by honoring and encouraging military service, offers scholarship opportunities and other ways to donate.

Give an Hour
www.giveanhour.org
This organization is gathering mental health professionals nationwide to give an hour of their professional services each week to military personnel and their families. Specifically targets U.S. troops and families who are being affected by the current military conflicts in Afghanistan and Iraq.

Homefront America, Inc.
www.homefrontamerica.org
An all volunteer 501(c)(3) nonprofit charitable organization comprised of military service members, veterans, their spouses, and families who understand the hardships and challenges of families left behind when a service member is away serving our country.

Medical and Mental Health

Alcoholics Anonymous
www.aa.org
AA is a fellowship of men and women who share their experience, strength and hope with each other that they may solve their common problem and help others to recover from alcoholism.

American Disability Association
www.ada.gov
Information and technical assistance on the American Disabilities Act.

After Deployment
www.afterdeployment.org
DOD mandated stigma free mental health resource. Specifically focuses on behavioral health needs of post deployment service members.

Army Battlemind Training
www.battlemind.org
Provides videos and information on return and reunion issues, combat stress, and PTSD for service members and their families.

Blinded Veterans Association
www.bva.org
The BVA is an organization of blinded veterans helping blinded veterans. Through our service programs, regional groups, resources, and advocacy, we hope to make life better for blinded veterans. There is no charge for any BVA service and membership is not a prerequisite to obtain help.

Bob Woodruff Foundation for TBI
www.remind.org/
Social network and resource center for people experiencing a TBI and their family members.

Center for the Study of Traumatic Stress
www.usuhs.mil
An ongoing source of information and support about traumatic stress.

Deployment Health Library
http://deploymenthealthlibrary.fhp.osd.mil/home.jsp
This library provides service members, families, veterans and healthcare providers an easy way to quickly find deployment health and family readiness information. Site includes fact sheets, guides, products, and links to organizations and resources devoted to your health and welfare.

Department of Veteran Affairs-Women's Issues
http://www.vba.va.gov/bln/21/Topics/Women/index.htm
Women veteran's health and benefits information including sexual trauma, health benefits and other issues relevant to female veterans.

DOD Deployment Link
www.deploymentlink.osd.mil
This site provides a wide range of info and resources on deployment health and combat stress.

DOD Deployment Health Clinical Center
www.pdhealth.mil
Provides information and links to other sites addressing a wide variety of deployment related issues.

Environmental Factors VA Website
http://www.va.gov/environagents/
VA information about environmental agents that may affect the health of service members who have served in the Middle East.

Force Health Protection and Readiness
www.deploymentlink.osd.mil
Site is maintained by the Office of the Special Assistant to the Under Secretary of Defense for Medical Readiness and Deployments. It links to National Guard and Reserve web sites.

Military Homefront –Wounded Warrior Resource Center
www.militaryhomefront.dod.mil/troops/injuredsupport
The newly established Center is available for service members and their family members to call (800) 342-9647 or e-mail 24/7 to request support.

National Amputation Foundation
www.nationalamputation.org
The Foundation sponsors an "Amp-to Amp" mentoring program. Whenever feasible, an amputee member of our organization who has returned to a normal life visits the new amputee. Has a list of support groups for every state and offers booklets and pamphlets of special interest to the amputee. Also accepts donated medical equipment, which is then given out to anyone in need.

National Center for Post Traumatic Stress Disorder
http://www.ncptsd.org
A website filled with important information and resources if you are dealing with combat related PTSD of a family member.

National Mental Health Association
http://www.nmha.org/reassurance/MentalHealthWarMilitaryFamilies.cfm
Offers a great publication: Coping with War-related Stress: Information for Military families and communities

National Suicide Prevention Lifeline
www.suicidepreventionlifeline.org
The National Suicide Prevention Lifeline is a 24-hour, toll-free suicide prevention service available to anyone in suicidal crisis.

Northeast Center
http://www.northeastcenter.com/links_veterans_resources.htm
This rehabilitation center website offers resources as well as a brain injury glossary, TBI articles, and monthly newsletters. Great information for those experiencing a brain injury and the family members who love them.

Paralyzed Veterans of America
www.pva.org
PVA works to maximize the quality of life for its members and all people with Spinal Cord Injury and Disease as a leading advocate for health care, research, education, veterans' benefits and rights, accessibility and the removal of architectural barriers, sports programs, and disability rights.

TriCare
www.tricare.osd.mil
Health care program for active duty members and their families, retired service members and their families, National Guard/Reserve members and their families, survivors and others entitled to DOD medical care.

US Army Center for Health Promotion and Preventive Medicine
www.chppm-www.apgea.army.mil/dhpw/Population/combat.aspx
Official site with info about signs of combat stress and how to deal with the symptoms, as well as physician information, including A Soldiers Guide to Deployment Related Stress Problems.

United States Welcome Home Foundation
www.uswelcomehome.org
Applies traditional and alternative medicine to the reintegration of the returning warrior, addressing the physical, emotional, social and spiritual wounds of war.

Veterans Administration Health Care Enrollment
http://www.va.gov/elig/

Veterans Affairs Readjustment Counseling Service
www.va.gov/rcs
This free service provides counseling and referral to combat veterans. Some free services are also available for family members of combat veterans.

Vets 4 Vets
www.vets4vets.us
A non-partisan veteran organization dedicated to helping Iraq and Afghanistan-era combat veterans heal through the use of peer support.

Vet Health
http://www.vethealth.cio.med.va.gov/Pubs/Index.htm
Links to brochures and publications including a summary of VA benefits for National Guard and Reserve Personnel, and healthcare and assistance for U.S. Veterans of Operation Iraqi Freedom

Women Veterans Health Strategic Health Care Group
http://www.va.gov/wvhp/
This group promotes the health, welfare and dignity of women veterans.

Networking

CinC House-Operation Homefront's Community of Military Wives
http://www.cinchouse.com
The Internet's largest community of military wives and women in uniform. Also the home of a wonderful book, "Married to the Military" by Meredith Leyva and many other resources for military family members.

SGT Mom's
www.sgtmoms.com
"Military Life explained by a Military Wife!" An unofficial but fun site filled with relevant information and links presented in a clear, navigable way.

Blue Star Mothers
http://www.bluestarmothers.org
Designed for mothers who have, or have had children serving in the military. Good information easily arranged.

GROWW
www.Groww.com
GROWW is an independent haven for the bereaved developed by the bereaved. Message boards and resource listings.

4 Military Families
www.4MilitaryFamilies.com
Support groups, discounts, travel, housing, and deployment information.

The Military Family Network
www.emilitary.org
Works to connect community organizations with military families to provide needed services.

Old War Dogs
www.oldwardogs.us/
A blog site for "old dogs" to voice their opinion on war, society and life in general.

Non Profit Organizations

American Freedom Foundation
www.americanfreedomfoundation.org
This 501(c)3 was organized to honor veterans of America's armed forces and raise money and awareness for various veterans' organizations with special emphasis directed to welfare and educational issues facing those wounded in action, disabled, and families and children of veterans killed in action during Operation Enduring Freedom and Operation Iraqi Freedom.

American Red Cross
www.redcross.org

America Supports You
www.americasupportsyou.mil
America Supports You is a DOD program that provides opportunities for citizens to show their support for the US Armed Forces by connecting individuals, organizations and companies to hundreds of home front groups offering a variety of support to the military community, also connecting military service members and their families to home front groups that provide assistance.

Association of the United States Army
www.ausa.org
AUSA is a private, non-profit organization that supports America's Army – Active, National Guard, Reserve, Civilians, Retirees and family members. AUSA also provides professional education and information programs.

Disabled American Veterans
www.dav.org
DAV is an organization of disabled veterans who are focused on building better lives for disabled veterans and their families. The organization accomplishes this goal by providing free assistance to veterans in obtaining benefits and services earned through their military service.

Military One Source
www.militaryonesource.com
A 24-hour, 7 day-a-week referral service available to anyone who has been deployed or affected by a loved one's deployment. Includes counseling referral, and resources. Military resource can also be reached by calling toll-free 800-342-9647.

National Fatherhood Initiative
https://www.fatherhood.org/deployeddads.asp
This organization offers many resources for dads including tips to stay connected during deployment.

National Military Family Association, Inc.
www.nmfa.org
A private national organization designed to identify and resolve issues of concern for military families. Provides resources and advocacy as well as Operation Purple programs.

Tragedy Assistance Program for Survivors
http://www.taps.org
Online community support and volunteer opportunities for those who have lost a loved one.

Official Resources

Army
www.army.mil

Army National Guard
www.arng.army.mil

Army Reserve
www.army.mil/usar

Air Force
www.af.mil

Air Force National Guard
www.ang.af.mil

Air Force Reserve
www.afrc.af.mil

Marine Corps
www.usmc.mil

Marine Force Reserve
www.marforres.usmc.mil

Navy
www.navy.mil

Naval Reserve
www.navalreserve.com

US Coast Guard
www.uscg.mil

Coast Guard Reserve
www.uscg.mil/hq/reserve/reshmpg.html

Veterans Affairs
www.va.gov

Prepared Life: Ready for Next Time

Family Member Deployment Checklist
www.abanet.org/family/military/checklist.pdf
A volunteer lawyers group has prepared an excellent Family Member Pre-Deployment Checklist. It is designed for all families and includes record-keeping questions related to medical care, finances, etc.

Family Readiness Tool Kit
www.defenselink.mil/ra/familyreadiness.html
Resources such as the Family Readiness Tool Kit and Guide to Reserve Family Member Benefits Handbook in PDF format are available on this site.

State or Branch Specific Resource

Some states offer special programs for their military families. Look here to see if there are any extras for your home state. If not, maybe you can start a program specializing in the needs of your area. All states are encouraged to try the National Resource Directory where you can find local and regional resources for your specific area.

https://www.nationalresourcedirectory.org/nrd/public/
DisplayPage.do?parentFolderId=6006

Alabama
http://alguard.state.al.us/frp/family.htm
This portal the Alabama guard family program provides great resources for Alabama residents.

Alaska
Stories in the News- Ketchican, Alaska
http://www.sitnews.us/OurTroops/ketchikan.html
This site is designed to highlight Alaska Guard and Reservists and the military happenings in and around the state of Alaska.

Arizona
Arizona Governor's Council on Spinal and Head Injuries
www.azheadspine.org
Provides information, education, programs and services for people with spinal cord and head injuries and their families.

Brain Injury Association of Arizona
biaaz.org
The Brain Injury Association of Arizona (BIAAZ) is the only statewide organization in Arizona dedicated to enhancing the quality of life for people with brain injuries and their families and working to prevent brain injuries.

The New Song Center
www.thenewsongcenter.org
The New Song Center for Grieving Children and Those Who Love Them provides a support group program for grieving children, youth, young adults and their families following the death of a loved one. New Song Center also provides comprehensive grief education for volunteers, the community and mental health professionals.

California
California Department of Veteran Affairs
http://www.cdva.ca.gov/Default.aspx
Provides resources for California veterans on education benefits, home loans and job opportunities.

Colorado
National Veterans' Training Institute
www.nvti.cudenver.edu
Develops and enhances the professional skills of veterans' employment and training service providers throughout the United States. NVTI is funded by the DOL and specializes in training employers who hire veterans.

Connecticut
211.org
http://www.211ct.org/InformationLibrary/Documents/
ActiveMilitaryandTheirFamilies-ResourcesSupport.asp
Access this website or call 211 and you can be connected to many valuable resources for military families.

Delaware
Delaware Healthy Families' Initiative
http://www.dhmi.org/familyviolence.htm
A comprehensive list of shelters and resources for families in crisis.

Florida
Florida Homefront
http://www.dma.state.fl.us/family/
This comprehensive site links many resources and news designed for Florida military families.

Georgia
Georgia Guard Foundation
http://www.georgiaguardfamily.org/
Provides emergency relief funds and services for Georgia military members and their families.

Hawaii
MWR Hawaii
http://www.mwrarmyhawaii.com/home.asp
MWR Hawaii provides many great links and resources for families stationed in Hawaii. Links include information about public schools, off installation housing areas, and a discount and activity card for spouses of deployed service members.

Idaho
Army Community Covenant
http://www.acsim.army.mil/COMMUNITY_COVENANT/state/idaho.htm
The Army Community Covenant is designed to develop and foster effective state and community partnerships with the Army in improving the quality of life for Soldiers and their Families, both at their current duty stations and as they transfer from state to state. Provides links to scholarship opportunities for Idaho families as well as camp opportunities for military children and youth.

Illinois
Illinois Military Family Relief Fund
http://www.standingupforillinois.org/homefront/
military_family_relief_fund_info.php
This fund was established to support guard and reserve families that have been called to active status. The site includes links to many other organizations that support and assist military families in Illinois.

Indiana
Military Family Research Institute at Purdue
http://www.mfri.purdue.edu/content.asp?id=13
This site provides links to research regarding the effects of deployment, reunion and military service on families as well as links to Indiana specific resources.

Iowa
Iowa Enduring Families Reconciliation Program
http://www.iowanationalguard.com/family/EnduringFamilies.htm
This link provides details about a program provided for Iowa families that are transitioning back from active status.

Kansas
Manhattan Kansas Chamber of Commerce Military Rights Page
http://www.manhattan.org/index.asp?NID=149
This page provides details and links to many other Kansas specific websites that benefit military families. Includes information about: military tuition discounts for combat veterans, in-state tuition for family members, spouse employment and emergency relief.

Kentucky
Blue Grass Military Affairs Coalition
http://www.bmaconline.org/index.cfm/bmacfan_home.html
This Kentucky organization is a community civilian resource network
established to facilitate support for families and friends of military people
on active duty.

Louisiana
Soldiers Angels of Louisiana
http://soldiersangelsla.org/?p=349
Links to Louisiana resources and free offers.

Maine
**Maine's Department of Health and Human Services – Military
Resources**
http://maine.gov/dhhs/boh/veterans_resources.htm
Links to Maine specific resources for veterans and their families.

Maryland
DC Military
http://dcmilitary.com/
Offers many DC resources for military families including specific links
for different installations.

Massachusetts
New England USO
http://www.usonewengland.org/Site/support/links.htm
This comprehensive site includes links for information on relocation,
health and fitness, financial, Morale Welfare and Recreation, Local Post
and Base Exchanges and other New England organizations that work
with military families.

Michigan
Michigan Project Blue Star
http://www.michigan.gov/homeland/0,1607,7-173-23612_34175—,00.html
This comprehensive site set up by the governor's office, includes specific
resources by Michigan County. Also links to the Michigan National Guard
Family Program and Military Family Relief Fund.

Minnesota
**First Lady of Minnesota Mary Pawlenty's Military family Care
Initiative**
http://156.99.41.1/FamilyPrograms-asp%20pages/firstladysrchNew1.asp
A list of service groups throughout the state of Minnesota, who have
expressed a desire to provide military families with a wide selection of
volunteer services.

Mississippi
Mississippi Community Covenant
http://www.acsim.army.mil/community_covenant/state/mississippi.htm
This site includes details about summer youth camps, Strong Bonds
Marriage Enrichment Workshops and tuition assistance programs for
service members and family members in Mississippi.

Missouri
Parent Link – Missouri
http://extension.missouri.edu/parentlink/military.htm
Parent Link provides resources and research for helping your children
transition through deployment and reintegration.

Montana
Montana National Guard Family Programs Website
http://montanaguardfamily.org/html/index.php

Nebraska
Nebraska Veterans Aid Fund
http://www.vets.state.ne.us/index_html?page=content/benefits.html
This site provides information about the Nebraska tuition assistance
program, as well as Nebraska Veteran's Emergency relief fund.

Nevada
Nevada National Guard Family Program
http://www.nv.ngb.army.mil/family.cfm#services

New Hampshire
New Hampshire Governor's Office Military Resources
http://www.nh.gov/nhsupport/

New Jersey
State of New Jersey Department of Military and Veteran Affairs
http://www.newjersey.gov/military/admin/highlights.html
This site links to important news and resources for New Jersey military
families including family programs, ESGR and Vet hotlines.

New York
New York State Division of Military and Naval Affairs
http://www.dmna.state.ny.us/family/frg.php
This site links to New York's FRG corner.

North Carolina
Governor's Office Website with Resource Links
http://www.governor.state.nc.us/mil/

North Dakota
North Dakota Family Programs Website
http://www.guard.bismarck.nd.us/family/

Ohio
On the Ohio Homefront
http://www.homefront.ohio.gov/Home.jsp
An Ohio wide "safety net" designed to connect military families with needed volunteer services.

Oklahoma
Oklahoma State University's List of Military resources
http://journalism.okstate.edu/resources/military.htm

Oregon
Coalition of Troop Support
www.cotsupport.org
The Coalition of Troop Support was founded to assist military units and families from Oregon and Washington. The purpose of the Coalition of Troop Support is to bring independent groups together in order to combine efforts to support military families.

Pennsylvania
Mission Homefront for Children
http://www.center-school.org/homefront/
This collection of resources includes many links and ideas to help children cope with deployment, reunion and reintegration for Pennsylvania families.

Rhode Island
RI Salutes
http://www.risalutes.com/
This program is designed to recognize the contributions Rhode Island National Guard and local military make to the economy as well as their contribution to security at home and abroad.

South Carolina
Clemson University
http://www.clemson.edu/fyd/crises_resources.htm
This database of resources includes those for families in crisis as well as general resources.

South Dakota
South Dakota National Guard
https://sdguard.ngb.army.mil/default.aspx
This site links to news and important information for South Dakota National Guard members and their families.

Tennessee
East Tennessee Military Affairs Council
http://www.etmac.org/
Provides a list of resources as well as a calendar of events breaking news and links to information for all branches of service.

Texas
http://OperationOnceInALifetime.com/?page_id=2
Provides financial and moral support to military families in need.

Utah
United Way of Utah
http://www.unitedwayuc.org/find_help/military_resources.html
The United Way of Utah provides resources for military families as well as details about military entitlements.

Vermont
Vermont Guard
http://www.vtguard.com/famRead/links.htm
This site includes links and resources for Vermont service members.

Virginia
Military Family Support Centers
http://www.milfamsupcen.org/links.htm
Links to branch and region specific sources for Virginia military families.

Washington
Coalition of Troop Support
www.cotsupport.org
The Coalition of Troop Support was founded after coming in contact with many different projects that local businesses and citizens had created in order to assist military units and families from Oregon and Washington. The purpose of the Coalition of Troop Support is to bring all of these independent groups together in order to combine their efforts.

Branch Specific

Air Force
Air Force Aid Society
http://www.afas.org

Army
Army Emergency Relief
http://www.aerhq.org

US Army Wounded Warrior Program
www.aw2portal.com
The U.S. Army Wounded Warrior Program assists and advocates for wounded Soldiers and their Families throughout their lifetimes, wherever they are located.

Army (Aviation Only)
Army Aviation Association of America
www.quad-a.org
The Army Aviation Association of America is a not-for-profit organization with many constituencies to include Active Duty, Reserve Component,

Civilian, Industry, Retired, affiliated organizations, and friends of Army Aviation. Regardless of interests and motivations there is one indisputable and overriding focus that the AAAA membership would agree upon as its purpose: To Support the United States Army Aviation Soldier.

Army Reserves Online
www.arfp.org
The Army reserve portal offers multiple resources for families of Army reserve members.

Marines
Family and Friends for Freedom Fund, Inc
www.injuredmarinesfund.org
Organized exclusively for charitable purposes to provide financial aid to injured marines and their families, as well as post traumatic stress disorder cases from war as the need arises.

Marine for Life
www.m4l.usmc.mil/Public/m4lx/start.aspx
The mission of this program is to provide transition assistance to Marines who honorably leave active service and return to civilian life and to support injured Marines and their families.

National Guard
Guard Family Portal
www.Guardfamily.org
Online training for service members, as well as volunteers and family members of National Guardsmen.

Troop and Family Counseling Services for National Guard and Reserves
888-755-9355
The group of professional counselors is available 24 hours a day, year round to help make the transition from deployment to reunion easier. They specialize in marriage and relationship issues, stress and anxiety, depression, grief and loss and anger management. Six prepaid, face to face counseling sessions are provided per family.

Navy
Navy Marine Relief Society
http://www.nmcrs.org

Navy Safe Harbor Program
www.npc.navy.mil/CommandSupport/SafeHarbor
The Navy Safe Harbor Program has a coordinated and tailored response for its men and women returning from Iraq, Afghanistan and other areas of conflict with severe debilitating injuries.

General Resources

I'm Already Home
www.ImAlreadyHome.com
Elaine, author of three books to help military families through deployment and reunion, has set up this site for people to get information, order resources and share ideas through the blog. Sign up for the InTouch newsletter packed with ideas and information.

Reintegration Booklet
http://channing-bete.com
You'll find information to order the booklet "Reintegration: Beyond Reunion – A guide for service members and their families." Or call 1-800-628-7733 and ask for item number PS92753.

Deployment Guide
http://www.deploymentguide.com
Includes details for readjusting after a deployment.

Operation Healthy Reunions
http://www.nmha.org/reunions/index.cfm
A well written, informative and upbeat article that covers many areas of reunion.

Divorce
www.divorcenet.com
Military divorce, family law, and counseling. Source of articles and information.

Military.com
www.Military.com
Connecting you to the benefits of service. It's an amazing site filled with information pertaining to all branches of services. It's always kept current.

My Daddy Fights for Freedom and My Mommy Fights for Freedom
http://www.geocities.com/mydaddyfightsforfreedom
Gives children a realistic outlook about their parents' deployment and tools to help deal with their feelings.

We Serve Too! 2 – A Child's Reunion Book
www.weservetoo.com
A wonderful new book by Kathleen Edick and Paula Johnson that helps kids with their parent's return from deployment. Filled with delightful illustrations that accompany a truly caring message.

The Armed Forces Foundation
www.armedforcesfoundation.org
This Foundation is dedicated to providing comfort and solace to members of the military community through financial support, career

counseling, housing assistance and recreational therapy programs. Programs are offered to active-duty and retired personnel, National Guard, Reserve components and their loved ones.

Military Family Program
www.carlisle.army.mil/usawc/dclm/joint.htm
Provides information to military families worldwide, featuring over 460 links to information and assistance web sites.

Comfort for America's Uniformed Services
www.cause-usa.org
Recreation and entertainment programs for injured service men and women facing months of rehabilitation. These programs are designed to bring a bit of relaxation and fun but also help wounded warriors begin the normalization process and the re-entry to home and community as they take their long journey back to health.

Military Assistance Program Central
www.dod.mil/mapcentral
An Internet desk guide providing information for family program professionals throughout the Department of Defense.

Fisher House
www.fisherhouse.org
Supporting America's military in their time of need, we provide "a home away from home" that enables family members to be close to a loved one at the most stressful time — during hospitalization for an illness, disease or injury.

Foundation for Senior Living
www.fsl.org/about/vision/index.html
They strive to provide exceptional services, education and advocacy in order to preserve independence and enhance the quality of life for all seniors, adults with disabilities and their caregivers.

Green Gate Farm
www.greengatefarm.org
Horses helping soldiers transition back to real life.

Gold Star Wives
www.goldstarwives.org
An organization of widows and widowers whose spouses died while on active duty in the military services or as the result of a military service connected cause.

Hadlt.com Veteran to Veteran LLC
www.hadit.com
A Veteran based site to guide veterans through the Veterans Affairs process for filing a claim for "service connected disability compensation." Hadlt combines knowledge, skills, and experience of Veterans to provide Veterans the information and support needed to navigate the VA system.

Helping Heroes Foundation
www.hohf.org/links.htm
Provides funding, services, and volunteers to augment the support service members injured in either Operation Enduring Freedom (Afghanistan) or Operation Iraqi Freedom. This runs parallel to the initiatives identified in the U.S. Army Wounded Warrior Program (AW2).

Iraq War Veterans Organization
www.iraqwarveterans.org
Provides information and support for: Operation Iraqi Freedom Veterans, Global War on Terror Veterans, Operation Enduring Freedom Veterans, active military personnel and family members related to pre-deployment, deployment, and post-deployment issues. Also provides information and readiness education for service members and families about Operation Iraqi Freedom Deployment Readiness, PTSD, Health issues and Veteran Benefits.

Lawyer Finder
www.lawyerfinder.com
Provides access to information, news, articles and attorney profiles for over 200 legal topics. All topics are broken down by U.S. state and geographic regions, so that you can find a lawyer to represent your specific need.

The American Legion
www.legion.org
The American Legion is a patriotic, war-time veteran's organization, devoted to mutual helpfulness. It is a not-for-profit community-service organization. With over 15,000 American Legion posts worldwide, membership offers travel discounts, career assistance and networking.

Military Community Awareness (A Guidance Group Company)
www.4mca.org
MCA is an educational publisher and distributor of curriculum, videos, publications and products for all branches of the military (all depts.).

Military Spouse Resources
www.milspouse.org
Employment, education and relocation information aimed specifically at military spouses.

Military Homefront – Heroes to Hometowns
www.militaryhomefront.dod.mil/heroes
This program focuses on reintegration post deployment. Networks are established at the national and state levels to identify the needs of reintegrating families before service members return home. Military Homefront also works to coordinate government and non-government resources necessary for long term success.

Military Life History
www.militarylifehistory.com
Provides a location to record your personal military history.

Military Spot
www.militaryspot.com
This site has a wide-ranging array of resources for military people. Military news, photos and videos are updated daily, keeping viewers abreast of the latest military-related events. Interactive features (forums, photo and video uploads, and a military social networking community) allow users to actively participate, contribute and share. Military-related information is extensive, covering everything from bullets to benefits. And just about any military-related product or service can be found in the shopping section.

Military Spouse
www.milspouse.com
Resources regarding deployment, relationships, family, money, career/education, well-being and home management designed for military spouses. Also offers online support as well as a magazine subscription.

National Association for Uniformed Services
www.naus.org
Founded in 1968 to protect and enhance the earned benefits of uniformed service members, retirees, veterans, and their families and survivors, while maintaining a strong defense, and to foster esprit de corps among uniformed services personnel and veterans of the United States, through nonpartisan advocacy on Capitol Hill and with other government officials, NAUS is the "Service member's Voice in Government".

National Domestic Violence Hotline
www.ndvh.org   1-800-799-SAFE(7233)
NDVH is a nonprofit organization that provides crisis intervention, information and referral to victims of domestic violence, perpetrators, friends and families. The Hotline answers a variety of calls and is a resource for domestic violence advocates, government officials, law enforcement agencies and the general public.

National Veterans Foundation
www.nvf.org
Serves the crisis management, information and referral needs of all U.S. Veterans and their families through management and operation of the nation's only toll-free helpline for all veterans and their families. Public awareness programs shine a consistent spotlight on the needs of America's veterans and outreach services provide veterans and families in need with food, clothing, transportation, employment, and other essential resources.

National Veterans Legal Services Program
www.nvlsp.org
NVLSP is an independent, non-profit, charitable organization acting to ensure that the U.S. government honors the pact made with our 25 million veterans. Offers Advocacy and Training, Education and Publication, and Pro Bono Litigation.

Operation Military Kids
www.operationmilitarykids.org
OMK provides youth program opportunities for school age, middle school and teenaged youth and connects them to support resources where they live. Through OMK, Military Youth can participate in recreational, social & educational programs, learn leadership, organization and technical skills, receive assistance with school issues, attend single day or weekend camps and meet other youth who are also experiencing deployment.

Operation Restoration Lost and Found, Inc.
www.lostandfoundinc.org
They work to provide specialized, professional intervention and therapy to returning troops and their families. Specializing in PTSD, separation anxiety, bereavement and grief, Christian based.

Patriot Guard Riders
www.patriotguard.org
This organization attends funeral services of fallen American heroes as invited guests of the family. They show respect for fallen heroes, their families and their communities and help shield the mourning family and friends from interruptions created by protestors or group of protestors through legal and non-violent means.

Project Sanctuary
www.projectsanctuary.us
This Colorado organization provides therapeutic, curative, supportive and recreational services to veterans, active military personnel, their spouses and children in the leisure environment of the beautiful Colorado Rockies.

Salute America's Heroes
www.saluteheroes.org
Works to provide a way for individuals, corporations and others to help our severely wounded and disabled Operation Enduring Freedom and Operation Iraqi Freedom veterans and their families rebuild their lives.

U.S. Small Business Administration - Office of Veterans Business Development
www.sba.gov/vet
Their mission is to maximize the availability, applicability and usability of all administration small business programs for Veterans, Service-

Disabled Veterans, Reserve Component Members, and their Dependents or Survivors.

Sew Much Comfort
www.sewmuchcomfort.org
Provides adaptive clothing free of charge to wounded service members.

Soldiers' Angels
www.soldiersangels.com
A volunteer-led nonprofit, with over 20 programs supporting all branches of the U.S. Armed Forces. Sends letters, care packages, and comfort items to deployed service members while also supporting families at home. Provides assistance to wounded warriors, continues support for veterans, remembrances and comfort for families of the fallen, and immediate response to unique difficulties.

United We Serve
www.unitedweservemil.org
This is a faith-based organization whose mission is to adopt troops and their families during deployment. Through networking and facilitating with individuals and other organizations, United We Serve provides a wide variety of practical, hands-on support and resources for our troops and their families, and creates a broader community awareness of the sacrifices of our military and their families.

USO
www.uso.org
The USO is a private, nonprofit organization whose mission is to support the troops by providing morale, welfare and recreation-type services to men and women in uniform.

US Wounded Soldiers Foundation
www.uswoundedsoldiers.com
Their mission is to provide for the needs of our combat veterans deployed in Iraq and Afghanistan.

Veterans of Foreign Wars
www.vfw.org
VFW's mission is to "honor the dead by helping the living" through veterans' service, community service, national security and a strong national defense.

Wounded Warrior Project
www.woundedwarriorproject.org
Wounded Warrior Project works to raise awareness and enlist the public's aid for the needs of severely injured service members and to help severely injured service members assist each other. Also provides unique, direct programs and services to meet the needs of severely injured service members.

Zero to Three
http://www.zerotothree.org/site/PageServer?pagename=key_military
This site is specifically designed to provide resources for military families with children ages zero to three. It includes great details about what your young children may experience throughout deployment and reintegration.

Veterans
AMVETS
www.amvets.org
Veteran support and community service opportunities

U.S. Vets
www.usvetsinc.org
They provide housing, counseling, job assistance, and HOPE to thousands of homeless veterans each year. Our programs foster the skills necessary for every veteran to return to the community and remain self-sufficient.

VA Vet Center
www.vetcenter.va.gov
Vet Centers provide readjustment counseling and outreach services to all veterans who served in any combat zone. Services are also available for their family members for military related issues. Veterans have earned these benefits through their service and all are provided at no cost to the veteran or family.

Veterans and Families
www.veteransandfamilies.org
To help our Veterans get home both mentally and emotionally; help Veterans and their families raise happy, healthy children in a safe and stable environment where both parents are supportive and emotionally available; assist our homecoming Veterans and their families in successfully transitioning home from deployment and from military to civilian life; keep families together through the trials of homecoming; work in tandem with all government and civilian resources and agencies.

Vocational Rehab Program for Veterans
www.vetsuccess.gov
The purpose of this web site is to present information about the services that the Vocational Rehabilitation and Employment (VR&E) program provides to veterans with service-connected disabilities. The web site also provides information about vocational counseling available to active duty service members and veterans who have recently separated from active duty. You will also find information about vocational counseling and special rehabilitation services available to dependents of veterans who meet certain program eligibility requirements.

Military Discounts

The following businesses are known for offering discounts, but <u>not all locations may participate</u>:

Apparel

Aeropostale
The Buckle
The Children's Place
Dress Barn
The Finish Line
FootAction
Footlocker
Gadzooks
Goody's

Hot Topic
Jos. A. Bank
Jockey
Kid-to-Kid (Children's Consignment)
Kohl's
New York & Company
Pac Sun
Rack Room Shoes
Timberland Outlets (active duty only)

Auto

AutoZone
Big 10 Tires
Checker Auto Parts

Kragen Auto Parts
NAPA Auto Parts
O'Reilly Auto Parts

Restaurants

Applebee's
Arby's
A&W
Back Yard Burgers
Barnhill's
Burger King
Captain D's
Carl's Jr.
Chick-Fil-A
Ci-Ci's
Cotton Patch
Denny's
Dunkin' Donuts
Golden Corral
IHOP
Java Cafe
KFC
Long John Silver

Maggie Moo's
McDonald's
The Melting Pot
Pancho's Mexican Buffet
Panda Express
Papa Murphy's
Pat & Oscar's
Pizza Hut
Quizno's
Red Robin
Shoney's
Sizzler
Sonic
Taco Bell
Texas Roadhouse
Wendy's
Whataburger

Services

AT&T
California Cryobank
Geico

Jiffy Lube
Meineke
Sears Portrait Studio

Travel and Leisure

Amtrak
Beaches Family Resorts
Blockbuster
Camp Jellystone
Greyhound

Movie Theaters
Professional Sports Teams
Ripley's Attractions and
    Museums
Sandals Resorts

Other Products

Apple Computers
Bass Pro Shop
Champs Sports
Copeland's Sports
Dell
Dick's Sporting Goods
The Discovery Channel Store
Gander Mountain
GNC
Great Party

Happy Harry's
K-mart
Michael's
Play It Again Sports
Pure Beauty
Sally Beauty Supply
Spencer's Gifts
Sportsman's Warehouse
Suncoast
Wilson's Leather

Cell Phone Service Discounts for Military

Alltel: Log in to your account on Alltel's Website and change your profile e-mail address to your .mil e-mail address. Further information is available by dialing 1-800-ALLTEL1

Cingular/AT&T: Call 1-866-246-4852. You can also go online www.cingular.com/discounts.

Nextel: Call 1-800-639-6111. Has merged with Sprint. New customers should go to a Nextel store; existing customers can provide their information over the phone to get the discount.

Sprint: Call 1-888-703-9514 and reference "AAFES code #0109565715."

T-Mobile: New customers should call 1-866-646-4688. Current customers should go to www.tmobile.com/corpdiscount. Follow instructions to register for "My T-Mobile," and you'll get a temporary password.

Verizon: Call 1-800-922-0204.

───────────◆───────────

Remember the best way to utilize your military discount is to get in the habit of asking everywhere you go, every time! The more people ask, the more likely businesses are to recognize how many military customers they already have, and should want to keep. Do you know of other places that offer a military discount? Please let us know. Login at www.ImAlreadyHome.com and share what you know. For more information about updated discounts, you can visit http:// www.4militaryfamilies.com/militarydiscounts.htm.

Meet Our Contributors

Many people shared their lives, stories and expertise with you throughout this book. You caught a glimpse of who they are, and the following biographical information will let you look further into their lives.

Reunion: Prospect and Possibility article written for Elaine Dumler by Linda Engelman and used with permission. Linda has been married to a National Guardsman for 37 years. Just completing a three-year term as the State Lead Volunteer, she is the lead instructor for the CISM sponsored Trained Crisis Responder course in North Dakota. Linda has presented many times at the national Family Program Workshop. Holding a master's degree in clinical counseling, she has ten years college level experience in teaching and counseling. Available for public speaking on a variety of topics, Linda can be reached at 701-250-7207 or lengelma@bis.midco.net.

Mild Traumatic Brain Injury: A Survivor's Handbook was the source for much of the information in the short section on TBI. Everything was used with permission for which I'm grateful. The authors of the handbook, Mary Ann Keatley, Ph. D., Laura L. Whittemore and Theta Theta No Beta Group are writing a more extensive book on TBI. It is due out in Spring 2009. They are members of the Brain Injury Hope Foundation and information can be found at: www.BrainInjuryHopeFoundation.org. They may be reached at Brain Injury Hope Foundation, P.O. Box 1319, Boulder, CO 80306, 303-484-2126.

The Road Home for Christopher was written for Elaine Dumler by Rick and Debbie Anderson and used with permission. From Rick: "Since Christopher's death on December 4, 2006 in Iraq, our world and priorities have changed significantly. Not having Christopher physically with us has been difficult and at the same time we have been greatly blessed. Our decision to focus on the blessings and move forward has changed our lives, and quite possibly made us better people. If by sharing our experience we can help people become better prepared to help those who may find themselves in ours or similar circumstances, please contact us."

Rick and Kyle are available for public speaking and can be reached at: **Rick@DocAndersonFamily.com** or P.O. Box 3065, Longmont, CO 80501.

Our Journey Began with a Phone Call was written for Elaine Dumler by Erin Richardson and used with permission. Here's a bit about Erin. "I have been married to my husband, Matthew, for five years and we have a two-year-old son. My husband is an Infantry soldier and we have been stationed at Fort Campbell, Kentucky since being married. Right now I am a stay-at-home mom but hope to return back to school once things calm down. We are settling well back into life here at Fort Campbell, and Matt is just waiting on one last surgery which we are hoping will be in the next few months. In the meantime I just enjoy our time as a family and all being together."

Laying a Foundation of Understanding was written for Elaine Dumler by Lawrence Luck and used with permission. Beginning in 1973 with the 306th Medical Clearing Company, Lawrence has always been a combat nurse and/or medic and managed field hospitals and clinics. As a combat medical instructor he developed several medical devices and procedures for field use. When he was in the Coast Guard he was responsible for protection of the space shuttle and its crews. He operated with the Coast Guard special ops unit for the protection of primary assets. While in the 217th MI Co A, Lawrence was a counter intelligence agent for the U.S. Army, as a linguist and instructor. He is currently in the 118th Air Lift Wing, Med Group. He is proud to have served America in the following Operations:

- Operation Desert Shield/Storm
- Operation Iraqi Freedom
- Operation Enduring Freedom
- Operation Just Cause
- Operation Southern Watch
- Operation Anaconda
- Operation Noble Eagle

Footnotes and Permissions

1. The Hidden Casualties of War: Promoting Healing and Resiliency for Servicemembers and Their Families. A two-day symposium presented as a Partnership Project of The Deployment Health Clinic —Naval Hospital Pensacola & The Center for Applied Psychology—Department of Psychology University of West Florida.

2. Article—University of Michigan Study, August 19, 2007, conducted by University of Michigan Institute for Social Research (ISR). Online study found at: http://www.ns.umich.edu/htdocs/releases/story.php?id=5987.

3. Article—*The Denver Post* newspaper, The Associated Press, November 30, 2008, by Lolita C. Baldor.

4. "Mild Traumatic Brain Injury: A Survivor's Handbook" by Theta Theta No Beta Group, published by the Brain Injury Hope Foundation, P.O Box 1319, Boulder, Colorado 80306, www.BrainInjuryHopeFoundation.org.

5. ibid. footnote 4

6. HONORING THE FALLEN: US Military KIA, Iraq/Afghanistan—January 2008, BlueNC.com.

7. ibid. footnote 1

All ideas included within this book have been used with written permission by each contributor. Names have been used only where specific permission was given to do so. Special permissions are below:

1. Quote: "Resilient military families don't want to be rescued, they want resources so they can help themselves."—Gen Craig R. McKinley used with permission from his office.

2. Article—"The Road Home for Christopher" by Rick and Debbie Anderson was written for single use in the book *The Road Home* and is protected by the book's copyright. Rick and Debbie Anderson retain all other rights to their article for use in other publications.

3. Drawing—"Woman in Mirror" was designed for Elaine Dumler by Shannon Parrish, http:// cartoonsbyshannon.com/invite.htm. Rights to the drawing were purchased for exclusive use by Elaine Dumler.

4. Photo—Statue and branch seals at the Military Tribute Garden in Westminster, Colorado were taken by Elaine Dumler and used with permission from the City of Westminster Parks and Recreation.

About the Author

Elaine Dumler educates in her own unique way—through speaking. She is a wife and mother whose husband served in the Army National Guard between 1969 and 1975 before they were married. As a speaker her clients take her around the globe, and recognizing that the stress of separation is there even when the timeline is relatively short, she was particularly touched by what military families face with sustained absences. Incorporating methods she used to stay connected to her husband and son along with ideas garnered from over 500 military families throughout the country, Elaine created "I'm Already Home," (first edition) a book designed to help families discover unique and wonderful ways to stay connected and in constant communication when they are apart. This book was released the week we went to Iraq in 2003. Her second book, "I'm Already Home...Again," released in 2006, combines the best of the first edition with over 170 new ideas, 120+ resources and stories gleaned through speaking with hundreds more families these past years.

This third book in the series, "The Road Home—Smoothing the transition back from deployment" is written in the tradition readers have come to expect from Elaine and helps with many of the situations each family finds themselves in following reunion and reintegration. It is filled with ideas that have worked for others, stories from interviews, and over 200 resources designed to help.

Focusing on bringing her message and methods of family unity to military families throughout the country, Elaine's work has been featured in *Ladies Home Journal, The N.Y. Times* and over 40 other publications including six in foreign languages. She's been on TV (including MSNBC, FOXNews and the Montel Show) and radio (over 70 programs) to talk about the importance of keeping family ties stronger than ever and the connection strategies most effective in doing so.

She is honored to be the recipient of the ABC "7 Everyday Hero" award for establishing the "Free Flat Daddy®" project, and presented with fourteen special challenge coins, including President George W. Bush's Commander in Chief coin, to honor her work with families.

Committed to helping military families at home and abroad, Elaine has been traveling to military installations and family readiness conferences throughout the country with her reassuring strategies for families with one goal in mind: to make sure that every American deployed or on temporary assignment in the service of their country has the means available to be in the closest contact possible with their loved ones left behind.

How to Order Additional Copies

- FAX ORDERS   303-430-7679
- TELEPHONE ORDERS   **Call Toll Free: 1-866-780-0460**
- ONLINE ORDERS   www.ImAlreadyHome.com
- POSTAL ORDERS   Frankly Speaking
                                          6460 W. 98th Court
                                          Westminster, CO 80021
- LOCAL TELEPHONE   303-430-0592
- BULK ORDERS OVER 25   **Call Toll Free: 1-866-780-0460**

I'm Already Home...Again –
Keeping your family close
while on assignment or deployment .... $12.95 ea.

The Road Home –
Smoothing the transition back from deployment .... $14.95 ea.

- Ask for information on how to **sponsor books** to military families or Family Readiness Centers.
- Ask for information about **Quantity Discounts starting at 25 books!**
- Ask for information about bringing Elaine in to speak at your conference or briefing.

SALES TAX   4% will be added to orders shipped to Colorado addresses.

SHIPPING $3.00 for the first book and $1.75 for each additional book in same order. Call for lower shipping rates for quantities of books over five.

PAYMENTS ACCEPTED   Visa, MasterCard, Discover
                                           Government IMPAC card
                                           Orders through Central Contracting
                                             (CCR# on file)
                                           Personal Checks

QUESTIONS   Call Toll Free at 1-866-780-0460

CALL TOLL FREE AND ORDER NOW!
1-866-780-0460
You can also order online at www.ImAlreadyHome.com